ENGAGING EPHESIANS:

AN INTERMEDIATE READER AND EXEGETICAL GUIDE

ENGAGING EPHESIANS:

AN INTERMEDIATE READER AND EXEGETICAL GUIDE

JOHN DELHOUSAYE

GLOSSAHOUSE
WILMORE, KY
www.glossahouse.com

ENGAGING EPHESIANS:

AN INTERMEDIATE READER AND EXEGETICAL GUIDE

© 2018 by GlossaHouse

GlossaHouse, LLC
110 Callis Circle
Wilmore, KY 40390

Publisher's Cataloging-in-Publication Data

DelHousaye, John -
   Engaging Ephesians: An Intermediate Reader and Exegetical Guide/ John DelHousaye. - Wilmore, KY : GlossaHouse, ©2018.

   x, 118 ; 28 cm. (Accessible Greek resources and online studies series. Tier 3) Includes bibliographical references.

   Library of Congress Control Number: 2018931111
   ISBN: 978-1942697442 (paperback)

1. Bible. Ephesians--Translating. 2. Bible. Ephesians--Terminology. 3. Greek language, Biblical--Grammar. 4. Greek language, Biblical--Textbooks. 5. Bible--New Testament--Greek--Language, style.   I. Title. II. Series.

BS2695.55.D44 2018   227/.5077

The fonts used to create this work are available from www.linguistsoftware.com/lgku.htm.

Book Design and Typesetting by John DelHousaye and Fredrick J. Long.

Cover Design by T. Michael W. Halcomb.

CONTENTS

AGROS

ACCESSIBLE GREEK RESOURCES AND ONLINE STUDIES

SERIES EDITORS

T. Michael W. Halcomb
Fredrick J. Long

GLOSSAHOUSE
WILMORE, KY

AGROS

The Greek term ἀγρός is a field where seeds are planted and growth occurs. It also can denote a small village or community that forms around such a field. The type of community envisioned here is one that attends to Holy Scripture, particularly one that encourages the use of biblical Greek. Accessible Greek Resources and Online Studies (AGROS) is a tiered curriculum suite featuring innovative readers, grammars, specialized studies, and other exegetical resources to encour-age and foster the exegetical use of biblical Greek. The goal of AGROS is to facilitate the creation and publication of innovative, accessible, and affordable print and digital resources for the exposition of Scripture within the context of the global church. The AGROS curriculum includes five tiers, and each tier is indicated on the book's cover: Tier 1 (Beginning I), Tier 2 (Beginning II), Tier 3 (Intermediate I), Tier 4 (Intermediate II), and Tier 5 (Advanced). There are also two resource tracks: Conversational and Translational. Both involve intensive study of morphology, grammar, syntax, and discourse features. The conversational track specifically values the spoken word, and the enhanced learning associated with speaking a language in actual conversation. The translational track values the written word, and encourages analytical study to aide in understanding and translating biblical Greek and other Greek literature. The two resource tracks complement one another and can be pursued independently or together.

PREFACE

I originally wrote this textbook for our seminary students in their third semester of Greek. We also began a discussion of textual criticism in the second semester. There are surprisingly few resources for helping students work through commonly cited variants. The excellent commentaries by Bruce Metzger (1971) and Philip Comfort (2015) attempt to cover the entire New Testament and are therefore necessarily selective. For semantics, we usually began with *A Greek-English Lexicon of The New Testament and Other Christian Literature* (2000) that was lovingly nursed into maturity by the great Lutheran scholar Frederick William Danker (1920–2012). Our primary conversation partners for syntax were Daniel Wallace's *Greek Grammar Beyond The Basics: An Exegetical Syntax of the New Testament* (1996) and Constantine Campbell's *Basics of Verbal Aspect in Biblical Greek* (2008). They are part of the same series published by Zondervan, although the authors disagree in places (primarily concerning deponency and aspect). For a similar guide, I recommend William Larkin's *Ephesians: A Handbook on The Greek Text* (2009). Sadly, he recently passed (2014), but this work testifies to his academic excellence. Also, decades of fine instruction are reflected in Harold Hoehner's *Ephesians: An Exegetical Commentary* (2002). It has been a pleasure to work with Fredrick Long and Michael Halcomb at GlossaHouse. I want to thank Fredrick, who is preparing a commentary on Ephesians, for his careful reading and suggestions that improved this guide. Also, I am grateful for my teaching assistant, Corinne Bellars, for helping with the indices. I hope *Engaging Ephesians* serves students of Scripture well.

Engaging Ephesians is divided into fourteen weeks—according to the length of a semester in a typical two-semester academic year. However, I have attempted to explain the phenomena of the text so that it could be read on its own. (Professors who adopt this textbook will know that I have only dipped a toe in the exegetical sea.) At the head of each week's portion, significant people and terms are listed that will be discussed in the commentary. Then I provide a vocabulary list for all the words that occur fifty times or less in the Greek New Testament. After giving the unit of the Greek text of Ephesians in grey highlight using the *SBLGNT* with places of dispute noted within brackets, I discuss matters of literary structure, rhetoric, semantics, and syntax. Typically, smaller bits of information are communicated in footnotes.

ABBREVIATIONS

BDAG	Bauer, Walter, Frederick W. Danker, William Arndt, and F. Wilbur Gingrich. *A Greek-English Lexicon of the New Testament and Other Early Christian Literature.* Chicago: University of Chicago Press, 2000.
Byz	Byzantine Manuscript Tradition
ca.	*circa* = approximately
Cod.Alex	Codex Alexandrinus
Cod.Bezae	Codex Bezae Cantabrigiensis
Cod.Sinai	Codex Sinaiticus
Cod.Vat	Codex Vaticanus
d.	died
ESV	English Standard Version Bible
L&S	Liddell, H. G., and Robert Scott, eds. *An Intermediate Greek-English Lexicon: Founded upon the Seventh Edition of Liddell and Scott's Greek-English Lexicon.* 7th edition. Oxford: Oxford University Press, 1945.
ms	manuscript
mss	manuscripts
MT	Majority Text
NA^{25}	Nestle-Aland, *Novum Testamentum Graece*, 25th edition
NA^{27}	Nestle-Aland, *Novum Testamentum Graece*, 27th edition
NA^{28}	Nestle-Aland, *Novum Testamentum Graece*, 28th edition
NAS	New American Standard Bible
NET	New English Translation Bible
NRS	New Revised Standard Bible
NT	New Testament
OED	Oxford English Dictionary
OG	Old Greek
OT	Old Testament
P	Papyrus; this abbreviation will have the papyrus number in the superscript (e.g., P^{46})
SBLGNT	*SBL Greek New Testament*
s.v.	*sub verba* = see "under the word" as defined in the lexicon specified
TDNT	*Theological Dictionary of The New Testament*
TR	*Textus Receptus* ("Received Text")[1]

---

[1] The phrase technically designates the edition of the Greek New Testament printed by the Elziver Brothers in 1633; it generally designates not only the Elziver text but also its precursors (Erasmus, Stephanus, and Beza) or any similar text.

INTRODUCTION

I. AUTHORSHIP

Many scholars classify Ephesians as a pseudonymous or deutero-Pauline letter—written by a disciple in the apostle's name.[1] They emphasize differences in style and content. We do not find this broad skepticism before the late twentieth-century, when scholars became overly confident in their sleuthing.[2] Nevertheless, those who read Paul's letters in Greek may sense that Ephesians, Colossians, and Philemon are more like one another than the rest of Paul's letters. Philemon is comparatively short—placed at the end of the *corpus Paulinum* for that reason—and personal. The similarity is more stylistic. Ephesians and Colossians place everything in Christ, including the universe. Paul describes the church as the body of Christ in 1 Corinthians, the authorship of which is undisputed, but in Ephesians he is the head to which eventually everything must submit. We also find more realized eschatology (see especially Eph 5:14). How might we account for these differences?

Earlier arguments for pseudonymity suffered from a bias to view authorship as the work of an isolated genius. Paul had partners in ministry and often included others as co-senders for his letters. Timothy joins Paul in greeting Philemon and the Colossians, although the apostle is the speaker throughout the letters. There are many similarities between Ephesians and Luke's Gospel and Acts (see Col 4:14). He is a leader in the church, but also a co-member of Christ's body. The Holy Spirit could have impressed the mind of Christ into Paul internally and communally. The apostle appropriated tradition and possibly liturgical material. He (or a scribe) may also have adapted his style to conform to the norms of Asiatic rhetoric, the region to which Ephesians was dispatched.

The church frowned on the practice of pseudonymity. Jerome notes, "Tertullian, who lived near those times, mentions a certain elder in Asia, an adherent of the apostle Paul, who was convicted by John of having been the author of the book, and who, confessing that he did this for love of Paul, resigned his office of elder."[3]

A strong, academically responsible case can still be made for Paul's involvement with Ephe-

---

[1] The term "deutero-Pauline" occurs in H. J. Holtzmann, *Lehrbuch der neutestamentlichen Theologie*, 2nd ed., vol. 2 (Tübingen: J. C. B. Mohr, 1911), 195. Works that argue for the pseudonymous authorship of Ephesians include Ernest Best, *Ephesians* (Edinburgh: T&T Clark, 1998), 11–36; Andrew T. Lincoln, *Ephesians* (Waco, TX: Word, 1990), lix–lxxii; and Rudolf Schnackenburg, *The Epistle to The Ephesians* (Edinburgh: T&T Clark, 1991), 24–39.

[2] Harold Hoehner offers a seemingly exhaustive tabulation demonstrating this (*Ephesians: An Exegetical Commentary* [Grand Rapids: Baker Academic, 2002], 9–20).

[3] *Lives of Illustrious Men*, 7 (trans. Ernest Cushing Richardson, *NPNF* 2/6:), 363–64.

sians.[4] If the letter were a forgery written by someone indifferent or hostile to the apostle, this historical question would affect our interpretation of the letter in that what could be learned from Paul's other letters would be less relevant. But those who are reticent to accept Pauline authorship nevertheless see Ephesians as the work of a faithful disciple. Therefore, either view allows Ephesians to be read in the context of the whole Pauline corpus.

Paul sent Ephesians, Colossians, and Philemon at the same time. Since it is unlikely that Tychicus made two trips as a letter-carrier, his mention in both Ephesians (6:21) and Colossians (4:7) suggests the letters were written around the same time. The mention of Archippus also links Colossians with Philemon (Col 4:17; Phlm 2). Colossians presumes the existence of a letter to the Laodiceans (4:16), which is no longer extant. The apostle may have sent all four letters with Tychicus, Onesimus, and maybe others at the same time.

II. PROVENANCE AND DATE

Paul draws attention to his chains (see Eph 3:1; 4:1). Some manuscripts of Philemon add a postscript claiming Paul wrote from Rome during his first imprisonment in AD 62 (see Acts 28:16–31). The primary difficulty with this claim is the great distance the runaway slave Onesimus would have to travel to be with Paul in Rome. Paul asks Philemon to prepare him a room (v. 22), which suggests that after being released the apostle intended to visit Colossae. But Paul's intention, after coming to Rome, was to go further west to Spain (Rom 15:24). Therefore, some claim Paul was imprisoned in nearby Ephesus, writing ca. 55. Although Luke never mentions this event, Paul relates he fought with wild beasts in Ephesus (1 Cor 15:32) and experienced terrible affliction (2 Cor 1:8). These reminiscences may relate a serious imprisonment passed over by Luke. The matter lacks a clear solution.

Ephesus was a thoroughly Greek city, but with a strong Roman presence. It was made the capital of the province of Asia under Augustus in 29 BC (Dio Cassius, *Roman History* 51.20.6). Population estimates range from 100,000 to 250,000, making it the third largest city in the Empire after Rome and Alexandria. Inscriptions attest to the wealth of many Ephesians. The city was especially proud of its role as "temple keeper" of Artemis (Strabo, *Geography* 14.1.22–23; Xenophon, *The Ephesians* 1.2.2–7). Luke records a riot involving Paul over the goddess (Acts 19). The conflict exposes massive spiritual conflict in the region (see Eph 6:12).

There was a large Jewish colony in Ephesus (Josephus, *Ant.* 14.225–27; 16.162–173). Presumably, many Jews were initially taken to the city as slaves. Their presence may explain why the apostle unpacks the implications for racial reconciliation between Jews and Gentiles (Eph 2:11–3:13).

---

[4] Markus Barth, *Ephesians: Introduction, Translation, and Commentary on Chapters 1–3* (Garden City, NY: Doubleday, 1974), 36–49; Hoehner, *Ephesians*, 2–60.

III. SOURCES

The apostle draws on the biblical (and post-biblical) **wisdom tradition** and cites from the **Mosaic Law** (5:31 / Gen 2:24; 6:2–3 / Deut 5:16), the **Prophets** (2:17 / Isa 52:7 and 57:19; 4:25 / Zech 8:16), and **Psalms** (1:22 / Ps 8:7; 4:8 / Ps 68:18; 4:26 / Ps 4:5).[5] This conforms to the **threefold Palestinian collection of Ancient Israelite Scripture**. Paul also echoes **Jesus Tradition** (e.g., 4:1 / Matt 11:28–30), cites an (apparently authoritative) tradition that is no longer extant (5:14), and mentions a brief letter he wrote, which the readers could consult, but may or may not have survived (see note at 3:4).

IV. OCCASION

In contrast to Paul's earlier letters, Ephesians is more general, approximating a summation of his gospel. The letter, which in many ways is more like a liturgical tract, with its many prayers, was probably intended to function as catechesis (a discipleship manual) to guide new believer from or to baptism (4:5, 22, 24, 31; 6:11).[6] The recipients are called "Gentiles" (2:11; 3:1), but are then instructed to live no longer as such (4:17). Paul paints a picture of what exodus might look like if Egypt were Rome and Pharaoh the Roman Emperor. But the apostle emphasizes the deeper spiritual dimensions of Paganism. What does new life in Christ look like? Having been freed from enslavement to sin, how shall we then live? The key word is power—the Creator's singular authority—available to us in Christ.

V. GENRE AND STRUCTURE OF PAUL'S LETTERS

All of Paul's extant writings are a kind of Greco-Roman letter.[7] The genre allows separated parties to communicate. Ephesians is most letter-like in its opening and closing greetings. Paul's letters have an Opening, Body, and Closing. Like a sandwich, the enclosing bread is greetings and prayers.

A. OPENING

The basic Greco-Roman epistolary greeting is A to B Greetings! (χαίρειν). This can be variously embellished.[8] The apostle begins every letter the same way: his cognomen Paul (Παῦλος). This nickname, often third in a series, was taken from a unique physical attribute or achievement. For example, Nero's birth to adoption name was Lucius Domitius Ahenobarbus. Ahenobarbus means "red-beard." In Latin Paul (*Paulus*) means "small." So the great apostle, perhaps originally named

---

[5] This is a striking contrast with the very similar letter Colossians, which does not cite any Scripture.

[6] The title "catechumen" came to refer to candidates for baptism after the process was extended in the early church to avoid apostasy or postbaptismal sin.

[7] This was the basic insight of Adolf Deissmann, although he wrongly separated "letters" (real letters) from "epistles" (non-real or literary letters). See Stanley K. Stowers, *Letter Writing in Greco-Roman Antiquity* (Louisville: Westminster John Knox, 1986), 18.

[8] Stowers, *Letter Writing in Greco-Roman Antiquity*, 20.

after King Saul (Hebrew *Sha'ul*), the tallest of his generation, introduces himself as "small one."[9] Paul may adapt the Greco-Roman greeting χαίρειν with χάρις "grace." Jewish letters from roughly the same period have *shalom* ("peace"):

Simeon, son of Kosiba, the ruler over Israel, to Jonathan and Masabbala, peace![10]

The apostle may join these elements into a new greeting:

χάρις ὑμῖν καὶ εἰρήνη ἀπὸ θεοῦ πατρὸς ἡμῶν καὶ κυρίου Ἰησοῦ Χριστοῦ (Eph 1:2).

Grace and peace may have a cause and effect relationship. Grace is God's unmerited delight in us as his adopted children, which brings peace into every sphere of life. A change in reality—the divine and human relationship—may have encouraged a change in form.

Paul usually ends the opening with a prayer of thanksgiving (Rom 1:8–15; 1 Cor 1:4–9; Phil 1:3–11; Col 1:3–14; 1 Thess 1:2–3; 2 Thess 1:3–4; Phlm 4–6).

B. BODY

Paul often signals a transition to the body with a disclosure formula: "I make known to you" (Gal 1:11) or "I do not want you to be uninformed" (Rom 1:13). The transition to the body in Ephesians is less clear. After the thanksgiving (1:15–23), Paul begins an argument, although this seems too late.

The body typically addresses the exigence—a problem requiring the apostle's attention—and offers updates on the apostolic mission. There is usually a primary exigence that almost demands a response, but also ancillary problems related or tucked into the discourse.

The body is similar to a homily, as if Paul were preaching to the community. The apostle often moves from the "is" to the "ought." The English modal falls between "must" and "may," which is a helpful description of exhortation in a sermon.

C. CLOSING

The apostle often ends where he begins, with greetings and prayers (see Eph 6:21–24).

With this general schema in mind, we can take a closer look at the structure of Ephesians. Earlier studies emphasized a linear progression to the body, while recently there has been more attention given to chiasm.[11]

---

[9] Luke does not explain the origin of the cognomen. He simply transitions to it during the first missionary journey, beginning at Acts 12:9, just before he mentions the proconsul of Cyprus, Sergius Paulus (v. 7). This might have triggered the switch. For Paul's Benjamite heritage, see Phil 3:5.

[10] Joseph A. Fitzmyer and Daniel J. Harrington, eds., *A Manual of Palestinian Aramaic Texts* (Rome: Editrice Pontificio Istituto Biblico, 1994), 159.

[11] For an elaborate and possibly forced interpretation, see John Paul Heil, *Ephesians: Empowerment to Walk in Love for the Unity of All in Christ* (Atlanta: Society of Biblical Literature, 2007), 13-45. See also P. S. Cameron, "The Structure of Ephesians," *Filologia Neotestamentaria* 3 (1990): 3–17.

D. LINEAR STRUCTURE

1:1–2: Greeting

1:3–3:21: "Indicative" or doctrinal section

    1:3–23: Doxology and Intercessory Prayer

    2:1–3:12: Exposition of Salvation

    3:14–21: Intercessory Prayer and Doxology

4:1–6:20: "Imperative" section

    4:1–5:20: Unity

    5:21–6:9: Household Code

    6:10–20: Spiritual Warfare

6:21–22: Mission of Tychicus

6:23–24: Blessing[12]

E. CHIASM

A Opening Greeting (1:1–2)

    1) The faithful (1:1)

    2) Prayer for "grace" and "peace"

    3) Directed to "God our Father and the Lord Jesus Christ" (1:2)

        B Prayer on "mystery" of God's will and spiritual warfare (1:3–23)

            C Christ's Family: Gentiles and Jews (2:1–3:21)

                D Walking with God (4:1–5:21)

                    1. "Walk" (4:1, 17; 5:2, 8, 15)

                    2. Trinity (4:1–6 // 5:18–20)

            C' Christ's Family: Spouses, Children, Slaves (5:21–6:9)

        B' Spiritual warfare and prayer on "mystery" of the gospel (6:10–20)

A' Closing Greeting (6:21–23)

    1') The faithful Tychicus (6:21)

    2') Prayer for "peace" and "grace" (6:23–24, inverse order)

    3') Directed to "God our Father and the Lord Jesus Christ" (6:23)[13]

These structures are not necessarily contradictory. Indeed, they (perhaps unconsciously) reflect the diverse unity of Jewish and Gentile (Greco-Roman) ways of thinking.

---

[12] Adapted from Raymond E. Brown, *An Introduction to the New Testament* (New York: Doubleday, 1997), 621.

[13] Adapted from Heil, *Ephesians*, 38–42.

With chiasms, the emphasis usually falls on the center—in this case, a broadly recognized unit on walking (4:1–5:21).[14] Five of the seven occurrences of περιπατέω "I walk" occur in 4:1–5:21 (see also 2:2, 10). The section also opens and closes with Trinitarian language (4:1–6 // 5:18–20).

The center of the letter according to word count is the statement ὁ καταβὰς αὐτός ἐστιν καὶ ὁ ἀναβὰς ὑπεράνω πάντων τῶν οὐρανῶν, ἵνα πληρώσῃ τὰ πάντα, "the One who himself descended is also the One who ascended—far above all the heavens, that he might fill all things" (Eph 4:10).[15] This is a fitting center to a letter that emphasizes the realized eschatology of Jesus's glory at the right hand of the Father and our position in him.

VII. PARATEXT

Accents, breathing marks, punctuation, and chapter/verse divisions were gradually added to the manuscript tradition of Ephesians. Although helpful, this paratext is not infallible. An exegete knows the options.

A. IOTA SUBSCRIPT

A small *iota* is often written under the vowels *alpha, eta,* or *omega,* especially when they are final. It looks like a tail: τῇ (see Eph 1:1). However, in our earliest mss, the *iota* was written ad-script (e.g., τηι). Byzantine scholars in the twelfth-century introduced the iota subscript.

B. BREATHING MARKS

Every Greek word in printed New Testaments that begins with a vowel carries a breathing mark above the vowel. It looks like an English single quotation mark: e.g., ὅταν. With capital letters, the mark usually goes to the left: Ἐφέσῳ (Eph 1:1).

If the breathing mark looks like an opening quotation mark, it is called a rough breathing mark; and the speaker traditionally adds an "h" sound. This is called aspiration. A smooth breathing mark looks like a closing quotation mark; no sound is made: Ἰησοῦ (Eph 1:3). Aspiration in Greek died out before the NT. We do not find breathing marks in our oldest NT mss

C. ACCENTS AND RULES

The accents (τόνοι) originally marked rising and falling tone, but today they alert the reader to which syllable to stress. There are three kinds of accents: 1) acute (e.g., δώδεκα), 2) grave (e.g., καί), and 3) circumflex (e.g., Χριστοῦ). Accents may only be placed on the antepenult, third from

---

[14] B. J. Oropeza, *Jews, Gentiles, and the Opponents of Paul: The Pauline Letters* (Eugene, OR: Cascade, 2012), 235; John R. W. Stott, *The Message of Ephesians* (Downers Grove, IL: InterVarsity Press, 1989), iii. The center of Heil's chiasm is 4:1–16 (*Ephesians,* 43).

[15] The middle words are specifically ἵνα πληρώσῃ according to the NA[28] text with articles treated as individual words. I am grateful to my former student Theresa Baker for assistance.

last syllable; penult, second to last; and ultima, last. For example, δώδεκα has three syllables. The acute accent is over the antepenult.

Antepenult	Penult	Ultima
δώ	δε	κα

An acute—upward pointing accent—may occur over any of the three syllables: κυρίου, ὑπομονήν. But the antepenult may be accented only when the ultima is short (e.g., ος).[16]
A circumflex may occur over the penult (δοῦλος) and ultima (᾿Ιησοῦ), but not the antepenult. For example, with θεοῦ the circumflex is over the ultima; ἐσθῆτι, over the penult.

A grave may occur only over the ultima: e.g., καὶ, because of its function—to replace an acute accent in the last syllable of a word when the word is immediately followed by another word without intervening punctuation.

The accent of a word may change when it takes part in a sentence. When the ultima is accented with an acute, it changes to a grave, except when followed by punctuation or an enclitic, a word pronounced with so little emphasis that its accent falls on the previous word. For example, the accent remains acute in the phrase ἀδελφοί μου because the second word is an enclitic.

Accents on nouns are fairly stable. They generally do not change from the lexical form (spelling in a standard dictionary, usually the nominative singular). Accents on verbs are recessive—they usually fall on the antepenult: ἡγήσασθε, περιπέσητε, κατεργάζεται, λείπεται, etc.

We do not find accents in the NT manuscript tradition until Codex *Bezae* in the fifth-century.[17] It is unlikely that the original publication of Ephesians contained them.

D. PUNCTUATION

We find four punctuation marks in Ephesians: comma or "separator" (,), semicolon or colon (·), period or "full stop" (.), and question mark (;).[18] These are editorial decisions. Note the absence of an exclamation point.

1. COMMA

The English word comma (= Latin) is derived from the Greek κόμμα, referring to *something cut off* or "a short clause of a sentence" (L&S). The ancestors of the comma marked the number of breaths required to read a short passage or to signify a pause. Modern English uses the comma to avoid ambiguity.

---

[16] There are a few exceptions to this rule.
[17] Plato mentions acute and grave accents (*Cratylos* 399); Ephoros and Heraclides, the circumflex (fourth-century BC). But accents were not universally employed.
[18] See 4:9. There are remarkably few questions in Ephesians.

2. SEMICOLON

In modern English, the semicolon falls between the comma and period. The two or more parts must be grammatically equal, unlike the comma, which can link independent and dependent clauses. It is a stronger separator than the comma.

3. QUESTION MARK

The greatest interface between interpretation and punctuation is the question mark. If the author does not use an interrogative pronoun (τίς, "who" τί "what"), context must be determinative.[19]

VIII. TEXTUAL WITNESSES

Our base text is *The Society of Biblical Literature Greek New Testament* (*SBLGNT*), edited by Michael W. Holmes, which generally follows the Alexandrian textual tradition, especially the fourth-century codices Vaticanus (Cod.Vat) and Sinaiticus (Cod.Sinai). We also discuss (albeit briefly) most of the Byzantine variants—some which are not even marked as a variant. In my opinion, they are characteristic glosses and expansions. But it is important to include them because modern textual criticism has suffered from a bias against the Byzantine tradition (Byz).[20]

Ephesians is attested in the papyri, our earliest witnesses to the autograph (original):[21]

1:1–23	P[46]	4:16–29, 31–32	P[49]
1:11–13, 19–21	P[92]	5:1–6, 8–33	P[46]
2:1–7, 10–22	P[46]	5:1–13	P[49]
3:1–21	P[46]	6:1–6, 8–18, 20–24	P[46]
4:1–32	P[46]		

These witnesses do not impress me; the transcription is often sloppy (see, for example, the P[46] reading at 4:30). Also problematic were the variants in Codex Bezae (Cod.Bezae), an exemplar of the so-called Western tradition (see 3:1). In my opinion, Cod.Sinai, our oldest complete copy of the NT, is closest to the autograph.

---

[19] The acute accent distinguishes the pronoun from being indefinite (τις "someone" or τι "something").

[20] A distinctive of the NA[28] from earlier editions is its adoption of Byzantine readings.

[21] Philip W. Comfort and David P. Barrett, eds., *The Text of The Earliest New Testament Greek Manuscripts: New and Complete Transcriptions with Photographs* (Carol Stream, IL: Tyndale House, 2001), 8.

WEEK 1—EPH 1:1–2

Key Terms and people: unit, Stephen Langton, form, genre, greeting, nominative absolute, apposition, ellipsis, preposition, transliteration, source language, target language, Lindisfarne Gospels, genitive case, subjective genitive, head noun, secondary agency, overdetermined, substantive, article, superscript, optative mood

Vocabulary

Ἔφεσος, ου, ἡ – Ephesus

1:1–2—GREETING

[1.1] Παῦλος ἀπόστολος Χριστοῦ Ἰησοῦ' διὰ θελήματος θεοῦ τοῖς ἁγίοις τοῖς οὖσιν [ἐν Ἐφέσῳ][1] καὶ πιστοῖς[2] ἐν Χριστῷ Ἰησοῦ· [2] χάρις[3] ὑμῖν καὶ εἰρήνη[4] ἀπὸ[5] θεοῦ πατρὸς ἡμῶν καὶ κυρίου[6] Ἰησοῦ Χριστοῦ.

The first rule of exegesis is *to cut at the joints*, i.e., determining where the **unit** begins and ends and its relationship to the rest of the discourse.[7] Some exegetes use the terms "pericope," "paragraph," or "stanza." We are attempting to discern the basic unit of human thought and expression that is semi-autonomous from its context. Such units are ideal for expositional preaching or teaching.

As we noted, the earliest mss of the Greek NT lack punctuation or versification. **Stephen Langton** (1150–1228), Archbishop of Canterbury, created the chapter divisions ca. 1205, using the Vulgate. His system was inserted into Greek mss of the NT in the fifteenth-century.[8] Langton's decisions are often sagacious, but occasionally obscure the flow of the text. He did not seem to be aware of *inclusio* or chiasm, important framing devices in both Testaments.

One way to cut at the joints is to identify the unit's **form** or **genre**. Some exegetes treat "form" and "genre" as synonyms. A *form*, as the word suggests, gives shape to a unit. It is not what the unit is, ontologically speaking, but what contributes to its existence. An example would be a cement

---

[1] This prepositional phrase is placed in brackets within the *SBLGNT*.

[2] A substantival, verbal (-τος) adjective ("those who believe").

[3] = Latin *gratia* or "divine favor." See John Eadie, *A Commentary on the Greek Text of The Epistle of Paul to The Ephesians,* 2nd ed. (New York: Robert Carter and Brothers, 1861), 7.

[4] = Hebrew *shalom* or "health," "wellbeing": see Eadie, *Commentary,* 7.

[5] A Genitive of Source: "from" or even "out of."

[6] Jesus is called κύριος twenty-three times (1:3, 15, 17; 2:21; 3:11; 4:1, 5, 17; 5:7, 10, 17, 19, 20, 21; 6:1, 4, 7, 8, 9, 10, 21, 23 [2x]). He is master over all earthly lords (6:5, 9). The epithet often signifies Yahweh in the OT.

[7] For more on unit delimitation, see Michael J. Gorman, *Elements of Biblical Exegesis: A Basic Guide for Students and Ministers* (Grand Rapids: Baker Academic, 2009), 37–38; Raymond de Hoop, Marjo C. A. Korpel, Stanley E. Porter, eds., *The Impact of Unit Delimitation on Exegesis* (Leiden: Brill, 2008). I learned to cut at the joints from my grandfather, a butcher at Marconda's Meats in Los Angeles, California.

[8] Byzantine scholars had introduced "headings" (*kephalai*) by the fifth-century, but they reflected thought units while the philosophy of chapter divisions seems to be primarily spatial—the equivalent of a page.

form that gives shape to a sidewalk, but does not become part of it. *Genre* focuses on content—what the unit is. As we noted, Paul writes a **letter** (or epistle according to an older classification) that approximates a sermon. In so doing, the apostle is compelled to adopt a recognizable form to meet hearer (reader) expectations. Form is largely determined by culture; it is a social constraint. A genre is often trans-cultural. For example, we have a generally standard way to greet people in an email. It is the same genre as Ephesians 1:1. But the forms differ with the culture and setting.

The unit is chiastic:

Παῦλος ἀπόστολος
Χριστοῦ Ἰησοῦ
    διὰ θελήματος θεοῦ
        τοῖς ἁγίοις τοῖς οὖσιν [ἐν Ἐφέσῳ] καὶ πιστοῖς
            ἐν Χριστῷ Ἰησοῦ,
        χάρις ὑμῖν καὶ εἰρήνη
    ἀπὸ[9] θεοῦ πατρὸς ἡμῶν
καὶ κυρίου Ἰησοῦ Χριστοῦ.

The form determines the opening syntax: Παῦλος is probably a **nominative absolute**.[10] "Absolute" means the nominative is not modifying a conjugated verb in a clause, the most regular function of the case. (Compare with the genitive absolute).[11] Like other languages, a sentence is not the only sense unit in Greek.

Paul (Παῦλος), the sender, provides further identification or credentialing: ἀπόστολος. This is called **apposition** (Latin *apposition* = *ad* ("near") *positio* ("placement"), a grammatical construction in which two elements, generally noun phrases, are placed side by side, with one element serving to modify and define the other. In Greek, the apposition will adopt the case of whatever it is modifying—since Παῦλος is a nominative (see above), ἀπόστολος is a nominative. In English, we use a comma to separate the elements: "Paul, an apostle."

So Paul, the sender, identifies himself according to translations as an "apostle." The transliteration of the Greek ἀπόστολος into English suggests there was not a clear analogy between the **source language** and the **target language**.[12] We find the spelling "apostol" in **the Lindisfarnes Gospels**, the oldest (extant) translation of the Gospels in English (ca. 950, OED), which, in turn,

---

[9] A Genitive of Source: "from" or even "out of."

[10] Daniel B. Wallace, *Greek Grammar Beyond The Basics: An Exegetical Syntax of the New Testament* (Grand Rapids: Zondervan, 1996), 49–51. Another possible syntax is the subject of an implied sentence: "Paul, (an) apostle of Christ Jesus, (sends this letter) to the holy ones."

[11] There may be ellipsis: "(This letter is from) Paul."

[12] The target language is the language being translated to—the antonym of the source language, the language being translated from. See Basil Hatim and Jeremy Munday, *Translation: An Advanced Resource Book, Introduction* (London: Routledge, 2004), xx.

was derived from the Latin *apostolus* by dropping the suffix. So the word "apostle" was birthed from the Bible, with the sense of being sent by Jesus Christ. However, the translators wanted to preserve some uniqueness for the word, perhaps because of the foundational role of apostles.

ἀπόστολος Χριστοῦ Ἰησοῦ – The **genitive case** often limits the meaning of whatever it modifies. In this case, Paul wants to limit his apostleship as being from the Lord (see Gal 1:1). In English, we typically supply "of" to the genitive to convey subordination—Χριστοῦ is modifying ἀπόστολος. However, the genitive can convey many senses, depending on context. In this case, the implied action of the head noun ἀπόστολος implies the **subjective genitive**: "apostle (sent by) Christ Jesus."[13] This syntax can be identified when the **head noun,** the one modified by the genitive, implies an action. This is often the case when a verb has the same root—in this case, ἀποστέλλω ("I send"). The genitive, then, supplies the understood subject.

Χριστοῦ Ἰησοῦ – Variation in the order of Jesus's name and primary epithet, the Christ (Messiah), is common in the mss. We find both orders in the context without variants. On the one hand, Cod.Sinai (ΙΥ ΧΥ, *nomina sacra*) and most of the Byzantine tradition read Ἰησοῦ χριστοῦ. On the other, the *SBLGNT* follows the earlier reading in P[46] (ca. AD 175–225), which is also reflected in Cod.Vat, Cod.Bezae, and other mss. I favor this reading because it is earlier and (slightly) more difficult—"Jesus Christ" being the default. The order also fits a couplet pattern:

Χριστοῦ Ἰησοῦ (1:1)
Χριστῷ Ἰησοῦ (1:1)
Ἰησοῦ χριστοῦ (1:2)
Ἰησοῦ χριστοῦ (1:3)

We also noted the inverse order in the final Greeting. In any case, the sense is little affected.

διὰ θελήματος θεοῦ may convey **secondary agency**, which correlates with the subjective reading of Χριστοῦ Ἰησοῦ: Paul is directly commissioned by Jesus, *but with God's will.* In other words, Paul's apostleship is **overdetermined**—having more than one agency (a common phenomenon in Scripture).

τοῖς ἁγίοις – Paul goes on to identify the recipients as "the saints." Again, the form determines the syntax: The dative communicates the recipient like an indirect object in a clause.[14] The adjective ἅγιος is functioning as a **substantive**—like a noun, except that the quality is emphasized. In contemporary literature, ἅγιος refers to angels who enjoyed access to the divine throne room (see Eph 3:12).

In Koine Greek, it is best to avoid the classification "definite article" because there is no "indefinite article," making the binary opposition misleading. Modern linguistics uses "determiner,"

---

[13] William J. Larkin, *Ephesians: A Handbook on The Greek Text* (Waco, TX: Baylor University Press, 2009), 1.
[14] Larkin, *Ephesians,* 2.

but the traditional **article** may be retained. In this case, the article functions as a "substantivizer" for the adjective ἅγιος.[15] In other words, it helps the reader determine that the adjective is functioning like a noun (see above).

Next we come to a significant variant, one that might affect the accuracy of the book's title.

[ἐν Ἐφέσῳ] – Our earliest mss (P[46], the original hands of Cod.Sinai and Cod.Vat, and Origen) do not mention the city. The phrase ἐν Ἐφέσῳ is written by a different hand in a different color of ink in the margin of Cod.Sinai. The words are also in the margin of Cod.Vat.[16] We may interpret these facts at least two ways. The scribes noted an omission or made an emendation.

On the one hand, some argue the letter was intended to be an encyclical.[17] The content of the letter is more general, suggesting a broader application, with Tychicus serving as its carrier and reader throughout Asia Minor (6:21–22). However, this may result from the modulation of genre already discussed. Perhaps a scribe wanted to harmonize the letter with Colossians, which is closely related in style and substance and reads ἐν Κολοσσαῖς (1:1). If we omit τοῖς οὖσιν ἐν Ἐφέσῳ, we have a seemingly more harmonious τοῖς ἁγίοις καὶ πιστοῖς (see Col 1:2).

On the other, an Alexandrian scribe might have omitted the phrase by accident or in order to generalize the letter. A clearer example is the omission of τοῖς ἐν Ῥώμῃ at Rom 1:14 in some later witnesses. The use of οὖσιν without a predicate is anomalous (see Rom 1:7; Phil 1:1; 1 Cor 1:2; 2 Cor 1:1).[18] All extant mss have the **superscript** or heading ΠΡΟΣΕΠΕΣΙΟΥΣ.[19]

The mss do not provide an alternative location.[20] The wording and arrangement suggest a parallelism, conveying a dual citizenship:

$$
\begin{array}{ll}
\text{τοῖς} \quad \text{ἁγίοις τοῖς οὖσιν} & \underline{\text{ἐν Ἐφέσῳ}} \\
\text{καὶ} \quad \text{πιστοῖς} & \underline{\text{ἐν Χριστῷ Ἰησοῦ}}
\end{array}
$$

Although the reading ἐν Ἐφέσῳ is uncertain, I find no compelling reason to drop it. However, I am charitable to other viewpoints because of the ambiguity.

ἐν Χριστῷ Ἰησοῦ – Something must be said—no matter how necessarily incomplete at this point—about this evocative prepositional phrase. J. G. Machen claims, "Few things are more necessary for a correct understanding of the NT than a precise acquaintance with the common prepositions."[21] A **preposition** (Latin *praeponere* "to set before") usually comes before its object, *conveying its position vis-à-vis another element in the context*. In context, the position of

---

[15] Larkin, *Ephesians*, 2.

[16] Eadie, *Ephesians*, xviii.

[17] Eadie attributes the theory to Usher (*Ephesians*, xxiv).

[18] Origen struggled to make sense of it (Eadie, *Commentary*, xix).

[19] Larkin, *Ephesians*, 2.

[20] Marcion may have claimed the letter was intended for the Laodiceans, but no extant witness supports this.

[21] *New Testament Greek for Beginners* (Toronto, ON: Macmillan, 1923), 42.

being "in Christ" refers to our adoption into God's family, but also the mysterious analogy of a husband and wife become one flesh, as Christ, the groom, is united to the church, the bride (5:22–33). The phrase, which is at the center of the unit, will also structure the subsequent benediction.

The proper noun Ἰησοῦς is a **transliteration** of the Hebrew-Aramaic יֵשׁוּעַ "yeshua," a later form for the biblical יְהוֹשׁוּעַ. Such nouns often cannot be fully declined in Greek. In this case, the genitive and dative are identical in form.[22]

Implied εἴη – Paul may assume a present optative verb (εἴη) in his Greeting: "(May) grace and peace (be) yours . . ." Such ellipsis is common in greetings. The **optative mood** pushes the action into the realm of hope or wish. It was falling out of use in the Koine period and has been fully replaced by the subjunctive mood (Ὑποτακτική) in Modern Greek.

ἀπὸ θεοῦ πατρὸς ἡμῶν καὶ κυρίου Ἰησοῦ Χριστοῦ may also be translated "from God the Father of us and (the Father) of (the) Lord Jesus Christ."[23] Depending on which reading is original, Paul will emphasize God as Jesus's father in the next line (v. 3). But all the genitives may be governed by ἀπὸ (KJV, ESV, Turner, *Ephesians*, 9).

ACTIVITIES & QUESTIONS

1. How many of Paul's letters begin with Παῦλος? How does Paul most commonly identify himself, i.e., what are the most frequently occurring self-referential appositions in his letters?

2. Did Paul originally write ἀπόστολος Χριστοῦ Ἰησοῦ or ἀπόστολος Ἰησοῦ Χριστοῦ? Although the notes claim that "the sense is little affected," what is the difference in meaning between the orders?

3. Was ἐν Ἐφέσῳ in the autograph or added later? How will this decision affect your interpretation of the letter?

---

[22] However, we find the dative form Ἰησοῖ in the LXX.

[23] Erasmus adopted this reading (Eadie, *Ephesians*, 8).

WEEK 2—EPH 1:3–14

Key Terms: benediction, *inclusio*, sentence, Granville Sharp Rule, arthrous, anarthrous, middle voice, Robert Estienne, attendant circumstance, *recapitulatio*, articular infinitive, accusative subject of the infinitive, divine passive

Vocabulary

ἄμωμος – blameless, faultless	κληρόω – I choose (an heir)
ἀνακεφαλαιόω – I sum up, recapitulate	μυστήριον, ου, τό – mystery, secret
ἀπολύτρωσις, εως, ἡ – redemption	οἰκονομία, ας, ἡ – arrangement, management
ἀρραβών, ῶνος, ὁ – down payment, guarantee	παράπτωμα, ατος τό – wrongdoing, misstep
ἄφεσις, έσεως, ἡ – forgiveness	περιποίησις, εως, ἡ – possession
βουλή, ῆς, ἡ – purpose, plan	περισσεύω – I abound, overflow
γνωρίζω – I make known	πλήρωμα, ατος, τό – fullness
ἐκλέγομαι – I choose (for oneself)	πλοῦτος, ου, ὁ – wealth, abundance
ἐνεργέω – I work, be active	πνευματικός, ή, όν – spiritual
ἔπαινος, ου, ὁ – praise	πρό – before
ἐπουράνιος, ον – heavenly	προελπίζω – I hope beforehand
εὐδοκία, ας, ἡ – good pleasure, purpose	πρόθεσις, εως, ἡ – presentation, plan
εὐλογέω – I bless	προορίζω – I predestine, choose beforehand
εὐλογητός, ή, όν – blessed	προτίθημι – I plan, display, purpose
εὐλογία – blessing	σφραγίζω – I seal
καταβολή, ῆς, ἡ – foundation, creation	υἱοθεσία, ας, ἡ – adoption
κατενώπιον – before, in the presence of	φρόνησις, εως, ἡ – insight, understanding
κληρονομία, ας, ἡ – inheritance	χαριτόω – I bestow on freely

1:3–14—BENEDICTION

Like the greeting (1:1–2), the unit is delimited by form: a **benediction**.[1] The opening line—Εὐλογητὸς ὁ θεὸς καὶ πατὴρ τοῦ κυρίου ἡμῶν Ἰησοῦ Χριστοῦ—also occurs at the beginning of 2 Corinthians (1:3) and 1 Peter (1:3). Presumably, it was a part of the early Christian liturgy, taken and adapted from the synagogue and/or temple (see James 3:9; Pss 41:13; 72:18; 89:52; 106:48). The opening line may have been a "riff" to be elaborated by hymnists in local congregations. In any case, the unit has profoundly impacted Christian theology, from Irenaeus of Lyon to John Calvin.

The *berakah* may follow an A B A' B' pattern, moving from the eternal, salvific purpose of the

---

[1] Tob 13; 1 Macc 4:30–33; Luke 1:68–79; Eph 5:17.

Father (A, A') to its realizations in the Son (B) and Spirit (B'). However, students have found an extraordinary array of structures in the unit.[2] I see a Trinitarian shape to the unit, perhaps echoing Jesus's baptism affirming his sonship (υἱοθεσίαν, v. 5) and beloved status (τῷ ἠγαπημένῳ, v. 6).

Cutting at the Joints: The mediating work of the Holy Spirit may form an ***inclusio*** (Latin for "confinement" 1:3, 13), which is a tool for demarcation whereby a word, phrase, or clause is repeated at the beginning and ending of a unit. It serves like a paragraph break in English. Verse 15 offers a clear transition.

The *berakah* often functioned as a prayer for protection from harm.[3] The Lord's Prayer addresses this important element. The Holy Spirit, then, may surround the unit as the means of protection.[4]

The sense unit is a single **sentence** of 202 words, the second longest in the NT. Everything is grammatically dependent on the opening line. However, this classification is anachronistic: a sentence was not recognized as a syntactical unit until the modern period.[5] Instead, Aristotle speaks of a περίοδος ("going around something"), which "has a beginning and an end in itself, and a magnitude that can be easily grasped" (*Rhet.* 3.9.3 [1409a]). In any case, the piling phrases and clauses invite ambiguity.

A. 1:3–6—ETERNAL PURPOSE OF THE FATHER

[3] Εὐλογητὸς ὁ θεὸς καὶ πατὴρ[6] τοῦ κυρίου ἡμῶν[7] Ἰησοῦ Χριστοῦ,[8] ὁ[9] εὐλογήσας ἡμᾶς ἐν[10] πάσῃ[11] εὐλογίᾳ[12] πνευματικῇ ἐν[13] τοῖς ἐπουρανίοις[14] ἐν Χριστῷ, [4] καθὼς[15] ἐξελέξατο ἡμᾶς ἐν αὐτῷ[16] πρὸ καταβολῆς κόσμου, εἶναι ἡμᾶς ἁγίους καὶ ἀμώμους κατενώπιον αὐτοῦ [,][17] ἐν

---

[2] For other options, see Hoehner, *Ephesians,* 159–161; Charles H. Talbert, *Ephesians and Colossians* (Grand Rapids: Baker Academic, 2007), 41–42.

[3] Max Kadushin, *Worship and Ethics: A Study in Rabbinic Judaism* (Binghampton, NY: Global Publications, 2001), 117.

[4] Talbert, *Ephesians and Colossians,* 48–49.

[5] See Ian Robinson, *The Establishment of Modern English Prose in the Reformation and the Enlightenment* (Cambridge: Cambridge University Press, 1998).

[6] The *SBLGNT* does not mention that καὶ πατήρ is lacking in some mss, but it is discussed in the commentary.

[7] The genitive may convey possession or possibly subordination (Larkin, *Ephesians,* 6: Lord "over" us).

[8] τοῦ κυρίου conveys the familial relationship between the Father and the Son—the so-called Genitive of Relationship—see Wallace, *Greek Grammar,* 83); contextually, the same is probably intended by ἡμῶν. In neither case does possession fit. We have a familial relationship with the God of Israel through the Lord Jesus Christ.

[9] The nearest possible antecedent is the Son, but context requires it to be the Father, who blesses us "in Christ." Otherwise, the wording should be "in himself."

[10] The dative is instrumental (Eadie, *Commentary,* 13).

[11] Since εὐλογία is anarthrous, πάσῃ signifies "every" (contra KJV).

[12] The *alpha* spelling is required because the stem ends in *iota* (ι).

[13] The syntax is probably a Dative of Sphere ("within" or "in").

[14] "heavenly things" (so Chrysostom and Luther—see Eadie, *Commentary,* 15).

[15] The adverb conveys manner (Eadie, *Commentary,* 18–19) or is causal.

[16] Two later codices read ἑαυτῷ ("Himself") instead of ἐν αὐτῷ. The simple reflexive ἑαυτῷ makes the Fa-

---

ἀγάπῃ. ⁵ προορίσας ἡμᾶς εἰς¹⁸ υἱοθεσίαν διὰ Ἰησοῦ Χριστοῦ εἰς¹⁹ αὐτόν²⁰, κατὰ²¹ τὴν εὐδοκίαν τοῦ θελήματος αὐτοῦ, ⁶ εἰς²² ἔπαινον δόξης²³ τῆς χάριτος αὐτοῦ ἧς²⁴ ἐχαρίτωσεν ἡμᾶς ἐν τῷ ἠγαπημένῳ,²⁵

Εὐλογητός – This adjective only refers to God in the NT.[26] This is also the predominate use in the Septuagint (Old Greek), with the Greek translating the Hebrew passive participle ברוך. The suffix -τός attributes a passive verbal quality to the adjective, allowing the reader to supply "is" or "be":

> Blessed be the God and Father of our Lord Jesus Christ (ESV)
>
> Blessed is the God and Father of our Lord Jesus Christ (NET).

On the one hand, the language may exhort worshippers to bless God.[27] The verb εὐλογέω often means saying something commendatory—*speak well of, praise, extol* (Luke 1:64; 2:28). On the other, it may be a declaration of reality.[28]

ὁ θεὸς καὶ πατήρ – Attending to form assists textual criticism. καὶ πατήρ is absent in Cod.Vat, but this is almost certainly a scribal error because of liturgical parallels (see above). The epithet "God and Father" is otherwise broadly attested. This is a clear example of the **Granville Sharp Rule**, which implies that God and Father are the same person. The first singular noun is **arthrous** (with an article), followed by καὶ and an **anarthrous** (without an article) counterpart.[29] But this is also clear from the context. The καὶ may be taken as a coordinating conjunction or possibly an emphatic adverbial: "God *who is* also Father."[30]

πάσῃ εὐλογίᾳ πνευματικῇ – The adjective πνευματικῇ is slightly emphatic due to its placement, either predicate or anarthrous restrictive attributive (most likely). This adds weight to the possi-

---

ther's election more personally emphatic. This is probably a scribal error—omitting the *nu* (ν) in ἐν αὐτῷ.This is probably another Dative of Sphere ("in Him") or possibly Association ("with Him").

[17] The placement of the comma here or after ἐν ἀγάπῃ (as in the SBLGNT) is interpretive. See discussion under ἐν ἀγάπῃ below.

[18] The accusative conveys purpose.

[19] The accusative probably conveys purpose or possibly advantage.

[20] The personal pronoun may, on rare occasions, convey a reflexive meaning (Wallace, *Greek Grammar*, 324–25).

[21] The accusative conveys purpose or standard.

[22] The accusative conveys purpose.

[23] This is probably an Attributed Genitive ("glorious grace").

[24] Byz mss read ἐν ᾗ instead of ἧς. The relative pronoun ἧς may be attracted to the case of its antecedent.

[25] The original hand of Cod.Bezae and a few other mss add υἱῷ αὐτοῦ. This sort of addition is common in the manuscript tradition.

[26] Samuel Hulbeart Turner, *The Epistle to the Ephesians: In Greek and English, with an Analysis and Exegetical Commentary* (New York: Dean and Company, 1856), 10.

[27] Earlier grammars suggested an implied optative.

[28] Harold W. Hoehner, *Ephesians: An Exegetical Commentary* (Grand Rapids: Baker Academic, 2002), 162.

[29] Wallace, *Greek Grammar*, 270–90.

[30] BDAG s.v. καί.

bility of *inclusio* with τῷ πνεύματι τῆς ἐπαγγελίας τῷ ἁγίῳ (v. 13; see structure above).

ἐξελέξατο ἡμᾶς – The verb ἐκλέγομαι only occurs in the middle/passive form in our literature. The **middle voice** may convey self-benefit.[31] In the least, it casts a spotlight on the subject. BDAG gives the occurrence here the meaning *to make a choice in accordance with significant preference—select someone or something for oneself.*[32] The verb often takes an infinitive to complement or complete its action.

εἶναι – This is an adverbial use of the infinitive conveying *purpose* or *result*. Most translations convey the form: e.g., NAS/ESV "that we should be holy and blameless," which largely follows the KJV. Yet the latter is suggested by Paul's assumption that his readers are presently "holy" (1:1). However, the apostle may also have intended a continuum (purpose-result): we are "holy and blameless" and must remain so in God's presence.

ἁγίους καὶ ἀμώμους – The **anarthrous** adjectives emphasize quality.

ἐν ἀγάπῃ – The phrase may modify what proceeds or follows. **Robert Estienne** (Stephanus) (1503–1559) divided the NT chapters into numbered verses in 1551.[33] A converted Catholic, he began to publish Calvin's *Institutes* in 1553 in Geneva. It is perhaps not accidental that he followed the reformer's exegesis (see below).[34] The KJV follows suit. But Chrysostom, Theodoret, and Jerome attach the phrase to προορίζω. Today, the translations are divided:

> [4] just as He chose us in Him before the foundation of the world, that we should be holy and without blame before Him in love, [5] having predestined us to adoption as sons by Jesus Christ to Himself, according to the good pleasure of His will (NKJ)[35]

> [4] even as he chose us in him before the foundation of the world, that we should be holy and blameless before him. In love [5] he predestined us for adoption as sons through Jesus Christ, according to the purpose of his will. (ESV)[36]

προορίσας conveys an **attendant circumstance** to ἐξελέξατο.[37] Daniel Wallace notes:

> The attendant circumstance participle is used to communicate an action that, in some sense, is coordinate with the finite verb. In this respect it is not dependent, for it is translated like a verb. Yet it is still dependent *semantically*, because it cannot exist without the main verb. It is translated as a finite verb connected to the main verb by *and*. The participle then, in effect, "piggy-backs" on the mood of the main verb. This usage is relatively common, but widely

---

[31] Larkin, *Ephesians*, 7. Wallace classifies it as an Indirect Middle (*Greek Grammar*, 419–23).

[32] S.v. ἐκλέγομαι.

[33] The rare edition contains the Latin translation of Erasmus and the Vulgate. The OT was completed in 1571.

[34] Calvin has completed his commentary on the New Testament by 1555.

[35] See also the NET.

[36] See also the NAS and NIV.

[37] Larkin, *Ephesians*, 7.

misunderstood.[38]

In other words, the action of the participle is concurrent with the conjugated verb. This suggests that election and predestination are two sides of a coin. BDAG gives the occurrence here the meaning "decide upon beforehand"—*predetermine*.[39] This is similar to ἐξελέξατο ἡμᾶς ἐν αὐτῷ πρὸ καταβολῆς κόσμου. Such redundancy is typical of Asiatic rhetoric.

ἠγαπημένῳ (from ἀγαπάω) – The substantival participle ἠγαπημένῳ is in the perfect tense, which is perhaps the most emphatic of the tenses, and may convey what Constantine Campbell calls "heightened proximity," although this is disputed.[40]

B. 1:7–10—REALIZATION THROUGH HIS SON

7 ἐν ᾧ[41] ἔχομεν[42] τὴν ἀπολύτρωσιν διὰ τοῦ αἵματος αὐτοῦ, τὴν ἄφεσιν τῶν παραπτωμάτων,[43] κατὰ[44] τὸ πλοῦτος τῆς χάριτος[45] αὐτοῦ **8** ἧς[46] ἐπερίσσευσεν εἰς ἡμᾶς ἐν[47] πάσῃ[48] σοφίᾳ καὶ φρονήσει[49] **9** γνωρίσας[50] ἡμῖν τὸ μυστήριον τοῦ θελήματος[51] αὐτοῦ, κατὰ[52] τὴν εὐδοκίαν αὐτοῦ[53] ἣν[54] προέθετο ἐν αὐτῷ[55] **10** εἰς[56] οἰκονομίαν[57] τοῦ πληρώματος[58] τῶν καιρῶν, ἀνακεφαλαιώσασθαι τὰ πάντα[59] ἐν τῷ Χριστῷ, τὰ ἐπὶ[60] τοῖς οὐρανοῖς καὶ τὰ ἐπὶ τῆς γῆς· ἐν αὐτῷ,[61]

---

[38] *Greek Grammar*, 640.

[39] S.v. προορίζω.

[40] *Basics of Verbal Aspect in Biblical Greek* (Grand Rapids: Zondervan, 2008), 46–52.

[41] The antecedent is the "Beloved," Jesus Christ (v. 6).

[42] The original hands of Cod.Sin and Cod.Bezae and other mss read ἔσχομεν.

[43] The genitive conveys separation ("away from").

[44] The accusative conveys purpose or standard.

[45] The genitive is attributed ("rich grace"). Cod.Alex reads χρηστότητος "kindness."

[46] The antecedent is χάριτος.

[47] The dative conveys manner, answering "how?"

[48] πάσῃ modifies the anarthrous σοφίᾳ and φρονήσει, a logical plural, signifying "all."

[49] ἐν πάσῃ σοφίᾳ καὶ φρονήσει modifies either the manner of the giver or recipients.

[50] Two later codices read γνωρίσαι. If original, this reading turns the sense to purpose ("in order to make known"). To my knowledge no modern translation has adopted this reading.

[51] The genitive conveys reference.

[52] The accusative conveys purpose or standard.

[53] αὐτοῦ is absent in Cod.Bezae and a few other mss.

[54] The antecedent is εὐδοκίαν.

[55] A later codex reads ἑαυτῷ.

[56] The accusative conveys purpose.

[57] "Stewardship" or "management": Paul normally applies this language to himself (1 Cor 9:17; Col 1:25).

[58] "Fullness"—i.e., "completion."

[59] "All things"—i.e., "creation."

[60] Cod.Alex and several other mss read ἐν. The more difficult reading has early attestation (the original hand of Cod.Sinai, Cod.Vat, and Cod.Bezae) and is therefore preferred. A second corrector of Cod.Sinai adds a τε before ἐν.

[61] ἐν αὐτῷ should be read with this clause, not the subsequent one in v. 11 (contra NRSV, ESV; see Hoehner,

ἀνακεφαλαιώσασθαι (from ἀνακεφαλαιόω) – This infinitive probably conveys purpose because of the parallelism with προέθετο ἐν αὐτῷ εἰς οἰκονομίαν τοῦ πληρώματος τῶν καιρῶν. The substantive adjective τὰ πάντα may function as the subject or direct object of the verbal action intended by the infinitive: 1) "that all things would sum themselves up in Christ" or "that he would sum up all things in Christ." The latter has broad attestation and fits the theocentric context (see KJV, NAS, NIV, ESV). The **middle voice** emphasizes the subject's role in the action, suggesting God's sovereignty in the determination (see v. 4). Paul uses the verb ἀνακεφαλαιόω once elsewhere to convey the rhetorical act of summing up an argument (Rom 13:9). A κεφάλαιον is the main point of a speech (Heb 8:1). So the most natural reading seems to be "summing up for himself all things." Bratcher and Nida paraphrase: "to cause everything that has been created to unite and to look to Christ as chief."[62] The image is new creation (restored Eden and cosmic temple).

After the apostles, **Irenaeus of Lyon** (died ca. 200) may be described as the church's first systematic theologian. He developed a theology of recapitulation in his magnum opus, *Against Heresies* (ca. 180). Irenaeus claims humanity was created like children—needing growth and education before they could live "according to the image and likeness" of the uncreated God (4.38). Given free will or "self-determination," we disobeyed and incurred humanity. Salvation, then, required two things: 1) reversing the consequences of disobedience and 2) leading people to perfection. God's engagement with humanity culminates in the incarnation as the *recapitulatio* (a "summing up"). He argues, "when he [Jesus] was incarnate and made man, he recapitulated [*or* summed up] in himself the long line of the human race, procuring for us salvation thus summarily, so that what we had lost in Adam, that is, the being in the image and likeness of God, that we should regain in Christ Jesus" (3.18).[63] Later, Irenaeus adds:

> This is why the Lord declares himself to be the Son of Man, because he recapitulates [sums up] in himself the original man who was the source from which sprang the race fashioned after woman; that as through the conquest of man our race went down to death, so through the victory of man we might ascend to life. (21.1)[64]

Throughout his work, we find the refrain, "the divine became human so that humanity might become divine" (3.10, 19; 4.20). In Christ, there is forgiveness and the grace for maturation.

Ephesians, 224). The redundancy of τὰ ἐπὶ τοῖς οὐρανοῖς καὶ τὰ ἐπὶ τῆς γῆς ἐν αὐτῷ emphasizes the finale.

[62] *A Handbook on Paul's letter to the Ephesians* (New York: United Bible Societies, 1993), 21.

[63] The translation is from Henry Bettenson, ed., *Documents of the Christian Church*, 2nd ed. (Oxford: Oxford University Press, 1967), 30.

[64] Bettenson, *Documents*, 32.

A. 1:11–12—THE ETERNAL PURPOSE OF THE FATHER

11 ἐν ᾧ καὶ ἐκληρώθημεν[65] προορισθέντες κατὰ[66] πρόθεσιν[67] τοῦ τὰ πάντα ἐνεργοῦντος κατὰ[68] τὴν βουλὴν τοῦ θελήματος αὐτοῦ,[69] **12** εἰς τὸ εἶναι ἡμᾶς εἰς ἔπαινον δόξης[70] αὐτοῦ τοὺς προηλπικότας ἐν τῷ Χριστῷ·

εἰς τὸ εἶναι ἡμᾶς – When the infinitive is the object of a preposition, it always takes an article and is an **articular infinitive**. The preposition εἰς in this construction conveys purpose. When there is also a subject, it will be in the accusative case.[71] We call this the **accusative subject of the infinitive**: "in order that we might be . . ."

προηλπικότας (from προελπίζω) – The perfect (active) participle conveys a stative point of view (aspect). The Christian life is forged and sustained in hope.

B. 1:13–14—REALIZATION THROUGH HIS SPIRIT

13 ἐν ᾧ καὶ ὑμεῖς[72] ἀκούσαντες τὸν λόγον τῆς ἀληθείας, τὸ εὐαγγέλιον τῆς σωτηρίας ὑμῶν[73], ἐν ᾧ καὶ πιστεύσαντες ἐσφραγίσθητε τῷ πνεύματι τῆς ἐπαγγελίας τῷ ἁγίῳ,[74] **14** ὅ[75] ἐστιν ἀρραβὼν τῆς κληρονομίας ἡμῶν, εἰς ἀπολύτρωσιν τῆς περιποιήσεως,[76] εἰς ἔπαινον τῆς δόξης αὐτοῦ.

ἐσφραγίσθητε τῷ πνεύματι – The Spirit is probably the secondary agency of the **divine passive**: The Father sealed us *with* the Holy Spirit. Amy Willis notes how the device "separates the subject

---

[65] Cod.Alex, Cod.Bezae, and a few other mss read ἐκλήθημεν "called."

[66] The accusative conveys purpose or standard.

[67] Cod.Bezae and a few other witnesses add τοῦ θεοῦ. Its addition is easier to explain than its omission.

[68] The accusative conveys purpose or standard.

[69] The genitive appears to convey the plan that results from God's will—a Genitive of Source or Origin (Wallace, *Greek Grammar*, 109).

[70] The genitive appears to convey the praise that will result from the revelation of God's glory—again, a Genitive of Source or Origin. The phrase is repeated from 1:6, perhaps forming *inclusio*.

[71] Wallace notes, "The accusative substantive frequently functions semantically as the subject of the infinitive. Though older grammars insist that technically this is an accusative of respect, from a descriptive and functional perspective, it is better to treat it as subject. This is a common use of the accusative, especially with personal pronouns" (*Greek Grammar*, 192).

[72] The second hand of Cod.Sinai and other mss read ἡμεῖς. The pronoun appears to be emphatic, emphasizing a contrast with the first person.

[73] A few mss read ἡμῶν.

[74] τῷ πνεύματι τῆς ἐπαγγελίας τῷ ἁγίῳ: The adjective ἁγίῳ is in the restrictive attributive position, perhaps emphasizing the holiness of the Spirit. The noun and modifying adjective are separated by τῆς ἐπαγγελίας.

[75] Cod.Sinai, Cod.Bezae, and Byz read ὅς. The reading may reflect development in the understanding of the Holy Spirit as a person of the Trinity. The neuter is attested by P[46], Cod.Vat, Cod.Alex, and other mss.

[76] ἀπολύτρωσιν τῆς περιποιήσεως is awkward to convey in English. περιποίησις may be translated "possession," and is probably functioning as an Objective Genitive: "the redeeming of (our) possession—i.e., the inheritance" (Larkin, *Ephesians*, 16). The understood verb is (ἀπο)λυτρόω. See 4:30.

of the verb from the doer of the action," rendering "the divine grammatically invisible as the doer of the action and this somewhat elusive as an agent within human history."[77] The action is overdetermined (review week 1). Of course, in this unit, Paul is drawing God's work into the light!

τῆς ἐπαγγελίας – F. F. Bruce essentially interprets the genitive as appositional: "the Holy Spirit is himself the promise of resurrection life and all the heritage of glory associated with it."[78]

ἀρραβών – The Greek is borrowed (transliterated) in Rabbinic literature: עֵרָבוֹן. It may refer to a payment of part of a purchase price in advance—a *first installment, deposit, down payment, or pledge* (BDAG; see Gen 13:17 LXX). Elsewhere, Paul presents the Holy Spirit this way (2 Cor 1:22). But the most likely background is protection.

ACTIVITIES & QUESTIONS

1. Cut at the joints in the unit. Where do you see any material cohering together? Feel free to consult commentaries until you find your structure.

2. Should we translate Εὐλογητὸς ὁ θεὸς καὶ πατήρ "Blessed is" or "Blessed be"? What are the theological implications?

3. John Calvin provides the following gloss on this unit. Evaluate his claims in view of your exegesis.

> The foundation and first cause, both of our calling and of all the benefits which we receive from God, is here declared to be his eternal election. If the reason is asked, why God has called us to enjoy the gospel, why he daily bestows upon us so many blessings, why he opens to us the gate of heaven,—the answer will be constantly found in this principle, that *he has chosen us before the foundation of the world.* The very time when the election took place proves it to be free; for what could we have deserved, or what merit did we possess, before the world was made? How childish is the attempt to meet this argument by the following sophism! "We were chosen because we were worthy, and because God foresaw that we would be worthy." We were all lost in Adam; and therefore, had not God, through his own election, rescued us from perishing, there

---

[77] Amy C. Merrill Willis, *Dissonance and the Drama of Divine Sovereignty in the Book of Daniel* (New York: T&T Clark, 2010), 70–71.

[78] "St. Paul in Rome: 4. The Epistle to the Ephesians," *Bulletin of the John Rylands Library Manchester* 49 (1967): 303–22, at 309.

was nothing to be foreseen . . . . If we view the word *love* as applied to God, the meaning will be that the only reason why he chose us was his love to men. But I prefer connecting it with the latter part of the verse, as denoting that the perfection of believers consists in love; not that God requires love alone, but that it is an evidence of the fear of God, and of obedience to the whole law. *Who hath predestinated us—* What follows is intended still further to heighten the commendation of divine grace . . . as the mercy of God is nowhere acknowledged in more elevated language, this passage will deserve our careful attention. Three causes of our salvation are here mentioned, and a fourth is shortly afterwards added. The efficient cause is *the good pleasure of the will* of God, the material cause is, *Jesus Christ,* and the final cause is, *the praise of the glory of his grace.* Let us now see what he says respecting each. To the first belongs the whole of the following statement *God has predestinated us in himself, according to the good pleasure of his will, unto the adoption of sons, and has made us accepted by his grace.* In the word *predestinate* we must again attend to the order. We were not then in existence, and therefore there was no merit of ours. The cause of our salvation did not proceed from us, but from God alone. Yet Paul, not satisfied with these statements, adds *in himself.* The Greek phrase is, εἰς αὐτόν, and has the same meaning with ἐν αὐτῷ. By this he means that God did not seek a cause out of himself, but predestinated us, because such was his will. But this is made still more clear by what follows, *according to the good pleasure of his will.* The word *will* was enough, for Paul very frequently contrasts it with all outward causes by which men are apt to imagine that the mind of God is influenced. But that no doubt may remain, he employs the word *good pleasure,* which expressly sets aside all merit. In adopting us, therefore, God does not inquire what we are, and is not reconciled to us by any personal worth. His single motive is the eternal good pleasure, by which he predestinated us. Why, then, are the sophists not ashamed to mingle with them other considerations, when Paul so strongly forbids us to look at anything else than the good pleasure of God? Lest anything should still be wanting, he adds, ἐχαρίτωσεν ἐν χάριτι. This intimates, that, in the freest manner, and on no mercenary grounds, does God bestow upon us his love and favor, just as, when we were not yet born, and when he was prompted by nothing but his own will, he fixed upon us his choice. The material cause both of eternal election, and of the love which is now revealed, is *Christ, the Beloved.* This name is given, to remind us that by him the love of God is communicated to us. Thus he is the well-beloved, in order that we may be reconciled by him. The highest and last end is immediately added, the glorious praise of such abundant grace. Every man, therefore, who hides this glory, is endeavoring to overturn the everlasting purpose of God. Such is the doctrine of the sophists, which entirely overturns the doctrine of Christ, lest the whole glory of our salvation should be ascribed undividedly to God alone.[79]

4. What are the strengths and vulnerabilities of Calvin's claims above?

---

[79] John Calvin, *The Epistles of Paul To the Galatians and Ephesians,* trans. William Pringle (Edinburgh: Thomas Clark, 1841), 178.

Key Terms: Thanksgiving, homoioarcton, direct object clause, attributive genitive, *nomen sacrum*, objective genitive, accusative of reference, the Old Greek, attributed genitive, conjunction, Lucian of Antioch, *Loci Citati Vel Allegati*, double accusative of object-complement

Vocabulary

ἀποκάλυψις, εως – revelation	μέγεθος, ους, τό – greatness
ἐνέργεια, ας, ἡ – working	μνεία, ας, ἡ – remembrance
ἐνεργέω – I work, accomplish	ὀνομάζω – I name
ἐπίγνωσις, εως, ἡ – knowledge	παύω – I stop
ἐπουράνιος, ον – heavenly	πλήρωμα, ατος, τό – fullness
ἰσχύς, ύος, ἡ – strength	πλοῦτος, ου, ὁ – wealth
καθίζω – I sit	ὑπεράνω – high above
κυριότης, ητος, ἡ – dominion	ὑπερβάλλω – I surpass
κληρονομία, ας, ἡ – inheritance	ὑποτάσσω – I subject
κλῆσις, εως, ἡ – calling	φωτίζω – I shine, illuminate
κράτος, ους, τό – might	

1:15–23—THANKSGIVING & INTERCESSORY PRAYER

This unit, a **thanksgiving**, is comprised of one period (= sentence) with 170 words.[1] Paul uses *inclusio*—τὴν καθ' ὑμᾶς πίστιν (1:15) // τοὺς πιστεύοντας κατὰ (1:19)—and employs a "latching device" by repeating the stem ἐνεργ- (ἐνέργεια and ἐνεργέω) in 1:19 and 1:20. The features allow two subunits:

1:15–19—Prayer of Request for *Visio Dei* ("Vision of God")

1:20–23—The Exalted Christ (object of *visio Dei*)

Paul prays for enlightenment in three areas, marked by the repetition of τί(ς): calling, inheritance, and power. Thanksgiving often leads to the body of the letter, although the transition here is unclear. Some view 1:20–2:10 as a digression.

---

[1] Larkin, *Ephesians*, 17.

1:15–19—PRAYER OF THANKSGIVING & REQUEST FOR *VISIO DEI*

¹⁵Διὰ τοῦτο κἀγώ, ἀκούσας τὴν καθ᾽ ὑμᾶς² πίστιν ἐν τῷ κυρίῳ Ἰησοῦ³ καὶ τὴν ἀγάπην τὴν εἰς πάντας τοὺς ἁγίους, ¹⁶οὐ παύομαι εὐχαριστῶν ὑπὲρ ὑμῶν ⸀μνείαν⁴ ποιούμενος ἐπὶ τῶν προσευχῶν μου,⁵ ¹⁷ἵνα ὁ θεὸς τοῦ κυρίου ἡμῶν Ἰησοῦ Χριστοῦ, ὁ πατὴρ τῆς δόξης, δώῃ⁶ ὑμῖν πνεῦμα σοφίας καὶ ἀποκαλύψεως ἐν ἐπιγνώσει αὐτοῦ, ¹⁸πεφωτισμένους τοὺς ὀφθαλμοὺς τῆς καρδίας ὑμῶν⁷ εἰς τὸ⁸ εἰδέναι ὑμᾶς τίς ἐστιν ἡ ἐλπὶς τῆς κλήσεως⁹ αὐτοῦ,¹⁰ [καὶ]¹¹ ⸀τίς ὁ πλοῦτος τῆς δόξης τῆς κληρονομίας αὐτοῦ ἐν τοῖς ἁγίοις,¹² ¹⁹καὶ τί τὸ ὑπερβάλλον μέγεθος τῆς δυνάμεως¹³ αὐτοῦ¹⁴ εἰς ἡμᾶς τοὺς πιστεύοντας κατὰ τὴν ἐνέργειαν τοῦ κράτους τῆς ἰσχύος αὐτοῦ[,]¹⁵

Διὰ τοῦτο – "For this (reason)" may refer back to the benediction, the preceding two verses with the switch to the second person, or it may anticipate what follows. The phrase may point both ways. Paul often uses the phrase causally (3x in Eph 1:15; 5:17; 6:13; see also Rom 1:26; 4:16; 5:12; 13:6; 15:9), a phenomenon we find elsewhere in the NT (Matt 6:25; 12:27, 31; 13:13, 52).

The sentence opens with a parallelism: (A) τὴν καθ᾽ ὑμᾶς πίστιν (B) ἐν τῷ κυρίῳ Ἰησοῦ καὶ (A) τὴν ἀγάπην (B) τὴν εἰς πάντας τοὺς ἁγίους. Paul maintains a close relationship between faith and love throughout his letters.

κἀγώ is a contraction (crasis) of the conjunction καί and first person personal pronoun ἐγώ. This contraction κἀγώ occurs twenty-five times in Paul's letters.¹⁶ The personal pronoun is unnecessary, but adds emphasis.

τὴν ἀγάπην – This noun is absent in P⁴⁶, the original hand of Cod.Sinai, Cod.Alex, Cod.Vat, and other mss and resulted probably from **homoioarcton** or "identical beginning" (τὴν . . . τὴν).

---

² Eadie found this phrase "peculiar" (*Commentary*, 75). It is an idiomatic expression for "the faith as it concerns you." κατά functions as *a possessive pronoun, with a limiting force* (BDAG). ὑμᾶς refers to Gentile believers.

³ As we noted, the Semitic name does not decline like a typical second declension noun.

⁴ Byz mss read ὑμῶν, which is probably a scribal clarification. The earlier, shorter, more difficult reading is preferred.

⁵ Possessive or Subjective Genitive = "while I pray." The preposition may have a temporal sense (Eadie, *Commentary*, 79).

⁶ Some treat δώῃ as an optative, which would be accented δῴη.

⁷ The *SBLGNT* does not alert readers that a variant reading occurs here. See the commentary.

⁸ εἰς τὸ + infinitive = purpose.

⁹ κλῆσις is a verbal noun (suffix –*sis*), signifying *an invitation to an experience of special privilege and responsibility* (BDAG). In Paul's letters, salvation is always the summons of God through Jesus Christ.

¹⁰ This is probably an example of a Subjective Genitive (Larkin, *Ephesians*, 21). God calls us to salvation.

¹¹ Not found in the *SBLGNT*, the addition of καί is a Byz reading.

¹² The dative conveys association: "among his holy (ones)"

¹³ The genitive is attributed: "surpassingly great power" (Larkin, *Ephesians*, 22).

¹⁴ This too is probably a Subjective Genitive (Larkin, *Ephesians*, 22).

¹⁵ The *SBLGNT* has no punctuation here; the NA²⁸ reads a period (see above).

¹⁶ Eph 1:15; Gal 4:12; 6:14; 1 Thess 3:5; 1 Cor 2:1, 3; 3:1; 7:8, 40; 10:33; 11:1; 16:10; 2 Cor 2:10; 6:17; 11:16, 18, 21, 22 (3x); 12:20; Rom 3:7; 11:3; Phil 2:19, 28.

This is a very common form of parablepsis: the eye jumps past whatever is between the identical beginnings.[17] This is an example of early reading that is nevertheless inferior.

τὴν ἀγάπην τὴν εἰς πάντας τοὺς ἁγίους – The Article "adjectivizes" the prepositional phrase, allowing it to occur in the arthrous restrictive attributive position with its slight emphasis.[18]

εἰς πάντας τοὺς ἁγίους – The preposition often conveys purpose, which fits the context: God's love was poured into our hearts for others. The arthrous τοὺς ἁγίους identifies a larger group than what was addressed in the greeting (1:1).

ὑπὲρ ὑμῶν – The preposition ὑπὲρ with the genitive case usually conveys benefaction (contrast with v. 22).

οὐ παύομαι εὐχαριστῶν is litotes, emphasizing a claim by stating its opposite. It is the equivalent of "I always give thanks." The participle here is complementary with the verb παύω. In the NT there are only a small handful of verbs that take complementary participles.

προσευχῶν – The noun προσευχή "prayer of request" anticipates a shift in the prayer form.

ἵνα often conveys purpose, as Eadie suggests, or result (or both).[19] However, the particle may also introduce a **direct object clause**. Wallace notes, "In this usage the direct object often follows a verb of commanding, urging, praying. The ἵνα clause thus gives the content to the main verb and in this respect answers the question *What?*"[20] Paul actually supplies his prayer.[21] The particle may be translated "namely" or the gist communicated by a dash.

ὁ θεὸς τοῦ κυρίου ἡμῶν Ἰησοῦ Χριστοῦ, ὁ πατὴρ τῆς δόξης echoes the opening line of the benediction (1:3). ὁ πατὴρ τῆς δόξης may be an **attributive genitive** and translated "glorious Father."[22] Wallace notes, "The genitive substantive specifies an *attribute* or innate quality of the head substantive. It is similar to a simple adjective in its semantic force, though more emphatic."[23] It is also called a "Hebrew genitive" because the earlier biblical language, like English, does not decline nouns into case forms. But, unlike our language, Biblical Hebrew allows a construct relation between a *status constructus* and *status absolutus*:

Status constructus	*Status absolutus*
Father	of glory
ὁ πατὴρ	τῆς δόξης

The epithet "Father of glory" does not occur in the Hebrew Bible. But we find δόξης for the *status absolutus* of גָּאוֹן ("eminence") and כָּבוֹד ("glory, splendor, honor") in reference to God in the

---

[17] Eadie describes the omission as a "blunder" (*Commentary*, 77).

[18] Larkin, *Ephesians*, 19.

[19] *Commentary*, 79.

[20] *Greek Grammar*, 475.

[21] Larkin, *Ephesians*, 19.

[22] The expression is unique (Eadie, *Commentary*, 82).

[23] *Greek Grammar*, 86.

LXX (OG).[24] It is probably not coincidental that the first occurrence is in the Song of the Sea (Exod 15:1–18), a paradigmatic praise form in Jewish piety, recited daily in the morning *shacharit* services.

πνεῦμα σοφίας καὶ ἀποκαλύψεως – The Fathers generally related the substantive to the Holy Spirit.[25] P[46] has the **nomen sacrum ΠΝΑ**.[26] According to Larry Hurtado and others, Christian scribes developed these abbreviations to mark out "sacred names."[27] Yet Paul can speak of a human spirit in concert with an unholy or Holy Spirit. πνεῦμα seems to be presented in parallel with καρδία (v. 18). The apostle may presuppose a tripartite view of human nature—body, soul, and spirit (see 1 Thess 5:23; Heb 4:12).[28] The difference is mitigated when we consider the human spirit as the recipient of the Holy Spirit. People are led by God's Spirit or the spirit of the world, which are antithetical to one another (see Eph 2:1–10). Both spirits may unite communities or even an age (Zeitgeist). We use terms like mob or herd mentality.

σοφίας καὶ ἀποκαλύψεως – This is probably hendiadys: "revelatory wisdom" (see note at 6:4).

ἐν ἐπιγνώσει αὐτοῦ – The substantive ἐπίγνωσις (-εως, ἡ) focuses on the transcendent in comparative literature.[29] What is apprehended is in the genitive case (αὐτοῦ). This may also be described as an **objective genitive**. The genitive provides the intended object of the implied action of the head noun. In this case, ἐπιγνώσει is related to ἐπιγινώσκω. It could be translated "in knowing him." The antecedent of the pronoun is Christ (Calvin) or, more likely, God the Father.[30] The dative is locative, limiting the wisdom and knowledge to "theology." Paul believes we may see the glory of the Father in the Son (Col 1:19; 2:9).

πεφωτισμένους τοὺς ὀφθαλμούς – The participle may be in the predicate position[31] and is probably an **accusative of reference**: "The accusative substantive restricts the reference of the verbal action. It indicates *with reference to what* the verbal action is represented as true. An author will use this accusative to qualify a statement that would otherwise typically not be true. This accusative could thus be called a frame of reference accusative or limiting accusative."[32] The perfect tense offers a stative viewpoint on the action that is probably a divine passive. The verb φωτίζω describes an inner or transcendent reality, being "enlightened" (BDAG).

τοὺς ὀφθαλμοὺς τῆς καρδίας – The **attributive genitive** limits the sense of the head noun, so that natural sight is excluded, unless a projection view is presumed. According to this assumption,

---

[24] See Exod 15:7; 24:17; 40:34–35.

[25] Eadie, *Commentary*, 85.

[26] Comfort and Barrett, *The Text of The Earliest New Testament*, 304.

[27] The significance of the *nomina sacra* is debated.

[28] This was a popular Jewish interpretation; see Josephus, *Ant.* 1.1.2. This language ocurrs in Philo and Talmud.

[29] BDAG s.v. ἐπίγνωσις.

[30] Eadie, *Commentary*, 86.

[31] Larkin suggests it is "a fronted attributive modifier of ὑμᾶς" (*Ephesians*, 21).

[32] Wallace, *Greek Grammar*, 203.

vision begins in the heart—today, we might say from one's worldview—and proceeds from the eyes and interacts with a light that comes from the object of focus, which then flows back to the eye and penetrates the heart where sight is registered.[33]

The second article τῆς may imply the presence of the personal possessive pronoun (ὑμῶν), despite being absent in P[46], Cod.Vat, and other mss, by "filling its slot." *When a substantive is modified by a possessive personal pronoun, it is usually arthrous.* But the article often takes this role by itself. The shorter, more difficult reading is preferred, contra *SBLGNT*. In any case, the sense is little affected.

τοῦ κράτους τῆς ἰσχύος αὐτοῦ – This is an **attributed genitive**, the reversal of the attributive genitive—when the head substantive is functioning like an adjective.[34] BDAG reflects this with its suggestion "mighty strength."[35] The slippery headship of genitives attests to the plasticity of the case. Context and semantics trump grammar.

1:20–23—THE EXALTED CHRIST

[20] ἣν[36] ἐνήργηκεν ἐν τῷ Χριστῷ ἐγείρας[37] αὐτὸν ἐκ τῶν[38] νεκρῶν, καὶ καθίσας[39] ἐν δεξιᾷ αὐτοῦ[40] ἐν τοῖς ἐπουρανίοις[41] [21] ὑπεράνω[42] πάσης ἀρχῆς καὶ ἐξουσίας καὶ δυνάμεως καὶ κυριότητος καὶ παντὸς ὀνόματος ὀνομαζομένου οὐ μόνον ἐν τῷ αἰῶνι τούτῳ[43] ἀλλὰ καὶ ἐν τῷ μέλλοντι· [22] **καὶ πάντα ὑπέταξεν ὑπὸ τοὺς πόδας αὐτοῦ**, καὶ αὐτὸν ἔδωκεν κεφαλὴν ὑπὲρ πάντα[44] τῇ ἐκκλησίᾳ, [23] ἥτις[45] ἐστὶν τὸ σῶμα αὐτοῦ, τὸ πλήρωμα τοῦ τὰ πάντα ἐν πᾶσιν πληρουμένου.[46]

καί in v. 22 is the first **conjunction** marking the break from one sentence to the next. Authors employ such particles *"to help keep an audience from wandering too far from the speaker's intend-*

---

[33] Mark F. Whitters, "'The Eye Is the Lamp of the Body': Its Meaning in the Sermon on the Mount," *ITQ* 71 (2006): 77–88.

[34] Wallace, *Greek Grammar*, 89–90.

[35] S.v. κράτος.

[36] The antecedent of the pronoun is ἐνέργειαν.

[37] The dative conveys means.

[38] A Byz reading lacks the article.

[39] Western and Byz mss present the action as a conjugated verb in the aorist tense (ἐκάθισεν "He seated"), which adds emphasis.

[40] The antecedent of the pronoun is the Father.

[41] This unique word occurred at 1:3 in a similar context.

[42] The preposition may be translated "high above" with a genitive object.

[43] The demonstrative pronoun is functioning like an attributive adjective, with the connotation of closeness. It cannot occur in the attributive position.

[44] The syntax is the same as the previous note.

[45] An indefinite form of the relative pronoun: there is nothing in the context to suggest an indefinite sense. This loss of distinction is common in Luke's writings (Luke 9:30; Acts 16:12; see Wallace, *Greek Grammar*, 343).

[46] This begins a trinitarian filling: the Son here, the "fullness of God" the Father (3:19), and the Spirit (5:18).

ed meaning while making it easier for the audience to recognize how the speaker intends for one statement to relate to a previous one (reducing 'process effort')."[47] It has a coordinating meaning, suggesting what follows is closely following on what precedes.

καὶ πάντα ὑπέταξεν ὑπὸ τοὺς πόδας αὐτοῦ – Paul offers his first citation from Scripture, from Psalm 8. The wording is probably from **the Old Greek (OG)**, although Paul's is slightly different.[48] The Old Greek is technically the more accurate way of referring to Greek translations of Scripture and other writings beyond the Pentateuch. Perhaps he cited Psalm 8 from memory. Later Christian monks memorized the Psalter. **Lucian of Antioch** (d. 312) wrote a commentary on the first fifty Psalms, employing a literal, historically conscious hermeneutic. He accepted as messianic only the Psalms read that way by Jewish exegetes—Psalms 2, 8, and 44.[49] This may explain the popularity of Psalm 8 in the NT. The NA[28] has a helpful appendix, *Loci Citati Vel Allegati,* that lists the citations from and allusions to the OT (Hebrew Bible) in the NT. According to this list, Psalm 8 is cited (noted by italics) four times (Matt 21:16; Heb 2:6; 1 Cor 15:27; Eph 1:22) and alluded to once (Rom 1:20).

καὶ αὐτὸν ἔδωκεν κεφαλήν – The substantive κεφαλήν is a **double accusative of object-complement**—"a construction in which one accusative substantive is the direct object of the verb and the other accusative (either noun, adjective, participle, or infinitive) complements the object in that it predicates something about it."[50] In this case, the pronoun αὐτὸν is functioning as the direct object of ἔδωκεν. Context identifies the antecedent as Christ. Paul, then, asserts he is the "head," echoing ἀνακεφαλαιόω in the benediction (v. 10).

ὑπὲρ πάντα – ὑπέρ with the accusative case generally conveys rank "over." Contrast with v. 16.

ACTIVITIES & QUESTIONS

1. Should we translate πνεῦμα σοφίας καὶ ἀποκαλύψεως as "Spirit of wisdom of revelation" or "spirit of wisdom and revelation"? What is the significance?

2. What is the difference between the Attributive and Attributed Genitive? According to Larkin, ὁ πλοῦτος τῆς δόξης τῆς κληρονομίας should be translated "rich glory of the inheritance."[51] Which position did he adopt, and do you agree?

---

[47] Stephanie L. Black, *Sentence Conjunctions in the Gospel of Matthew: καί, δέ, τότε, γάρ, οὖν and Asyndeton in Narrative Discourse* (Sheffield: Sheffield Academic, 2002), 56–57, emphasis added.

[48] πάντα ὑπέταξας ὑποκάτω τῶν ποδῶν αὐτοῦ (Ps 8:7 OG).

[49] John McGuckin, "Controversy and Councils: Greek theology, 4th–6th centuries," in *Christian Thought: A Brief History,* ed. Adrian Hastings, Alison Masin, and Hugh Pyper (Oxford: Oxford University Press, 2002), 17–32, 27.

[50] Wallace, *Greek Grammar,* 182.

[51] *Ephesians,* 22.

Key Terms: review of salvation-history, subunit, adversative conjunction, imperfect tense, genitive of destination, anadiplosis, anaphoric, postcedent, clausal antecedent, intensive perfect, English Present Perfect, the Majority Text

Vocabulary

ἀήρ, ἀέρος, ὁ – air, ethereal region above the earth	πλούσιος, ία, ιον – rich
ἀναστρέφω – I live	πλοῦτος, ου, ὁ – wealth
ἀπείθεια, ας, ἡ – disobedience	ποίημα, ατος, τό – work, creation, what is made
διάνοια, ας, ἡ – understanding, mind	
δῶρον, ου, τό – gift	ποτέ – formerly
ἔλεος, ους, τό – mercy	προετοιμάζω – I prepare beforehand
ἐνδείκνυμι – I show	συγκαθίζω – I let seat with
ἐνεργέω – I work	συνεγείρω – I raise together with
ἐπέρχομαι – I come	συζωοποιέω – I make alive together with
ἐπουράνιος, ον – heavenly	ὑπερβάλλω – I surpass
κτίζω – I create	φύσις, εως, ἡ – nature
παράπτωμα, ατος τό – wrongdoing, misstep	χρηστότης, ητος, ἡ – kindness

2:1–10—SAVED FROM SIN TO LIFE

This unit may mark the transition to **the body** of the letter, but καί continues the thought of the previous unit, repeating several words:

πνεῦμα (1:17 // 2:2)

ἐνεργέω (1:20 // 2:2)

νεκρός (1:20 // 2:1)

αἰών (1:21 // 2:2)

ἀρχή (1:21 // ἄρχων 2:2)

ἐξουσία (1:21 // 2:2).[1]

Indeed, Philip Comfort notes: "These verses [2:1–3], grammatically speaking, should be connected with the end of chapter 1, otherwise they are just dangling."[2]

The most dramatic repetition is Jesus's two-stage victory over death applied now to believers:

---

[1] Larkin, *Ephesians*, 27.

[2] *A Commentary on the Manuscripts and Text of the New Testament* (Grand Rapids: Kregel Academic, 2015), 341.

ἐγείρας αὐτὸν ἐκ νεκρῶν (1:20) = <u>συν</u>ήγειρεν (2:6)

καθίσας ἐν δεξιᾷ αὐτοῦ ἐν τοῖς ἐπουρανίοις (1:20) = <u>συν</u>εκάθισεν ἐν τοῖς ἐπουρανίοις (2:6)

The prefixed preposition σύν marks accompaniment or association. *Salvation comes from union with Christ*. Paul (or his source) had to create a new verb to capture this mystery.[3] A change in reality requires new vocabulary.

1:20–2:7 is a **review of salvation-history** (German *Heilsgeschichte*), like a more specific thanksgiving (*todah*) psalm we find in the Psalter, which generally includes a summation of the exodus story (105–106, 135, 136). Paul celebrates the "new exodus" from death and sin, which began in the Messiah and is being applied to his regathered, reconciling people.

Cutting at the Joints: The repetition of the verb περιπατέω forms *inclusio* (vv. 2, 10). Paul also divides the unit into two **subunits** (distinct components of a larger unit) with a before and after picture, marked by the **adversative conjunction** δέ at v. 4. According to Stephanie Black, the particle serves as a "marker informing the audience that in some respect continuity is not maintained at this point in the discourse."[4]

2:1–3—THEN

> **2.1** Καὶ ὑμᾶς[5] ὄντας[6] νεκροὺς[7] τοῖς παραπτώμασιν καὶ ταῖς ἁμαρτίαις ὑμῶν,[8] **2** ἐν αἷς[9] ποτε[10] περιεπατήσατε κατὰ τὸν αἰῶνα τοῦ κόσμου τούτου,[11] κατὰ τὸν ἄρχοντα τῆς ἐξουσίας τοῦ ἀέρος,[12] τοῦ πνεύματος[13] τοῦ νῦν ἐνεργοῦντος ἐν[14] τοῖς υἱοῖς τῆς ἀπειθείας· **3** ἐν οἷς καὶ

---

[3] συζωοποιέω does not occur in extant literature before Ephesians and Colossians. We find συνεγείρω in the LXX / OG (Exod 33:4; 4 Macc 2:14) as well as συγκαθίζω (Gen 15:11; Exod 18:13; 1 Esd 9.6; see also Luke 22:55).

[4] *Sentence Conjunctions*, 144. She warns about pressing the adjective "adversative" too far.

[5] The emphatic pronoun functions as the topic in a topic construction where the focal point of the unit is brought forward—in this case, from 2:5—for emphasis (Larkin, *Ephesians*, 27).

[6] The participle is functioning like an attributive adjective of ὑμᾶς (Larkin, *Ephesians*, 27).

[7] Predicate adjective of ὄντας with ὑμᾶς being the subject.

[8] Absent in Byz mss yet not recorded in NA[28] or *SBLGNT*. If original, the sense may be a Subjective Genitive ("you sin and commit trespasses"). But the simpler possessive makes sense.

[9] The relative pronoun adopts the gender of the nearer ἁμαρτία. Although παράπτωμα may also be part of the antecedent (Eadie, *Commentary*, 124), περιπατέω probably repeats the gist of παράπτωμα, forming a chiasm: A) παράπτωμα, B) ἁμαρτία, B') [ἁμαρτία = αἷς], A') περιπατέω. The form emphasizes "living (walking) in sin."

[10] The adverb ("formerly") is rhetorically significant, presupposing a moral transformation of the hearers. The alliteration (ποτε περιεπατήσατε) catches the ear.

[11] Context suggests αἰών signifies "age," not "world." Larkin treats τοῦ κόσμου τούτου as an Attributed Genitive, suggesting the translation "world-age" (*Ephesians*, 28). The demonstrative cannot occur in the attributive position because it is technically a pronoun.

[12] The sense may be Epexegetical—identifying the "domain" more precisely (Eadie, *Commentary*, 127; Larkin, *Ephesians*, 28). But the Genitive of Subordination makes sense here (Wallace, *Greek Grammar*, 104).

[13] With some interpreters one may have expected πνεύματος to be placed in the accusative case in apposition to ἄρχοντα; instead, it is probably in apposition to ἀέρος since "air" and "spirit" overlap semantically.

[14] ἐν may locate where the evil spirit is at work—*in*—or how—*by means*. The latter is intended by the earlier

ἡμεῖς πάντες ἀνεστράφημέν ποτε ἐν ταῖς ἐπιθυμίαις τῆς σαρκὸς ἡμῶν, ποιοῦντες¹⁵ τὰ
θελήματα τῆς σαρκὸς¹⁶ καὶ τῶν διανοιῶν, καὶ ἤμεθα¹⁷ τέκνα φύσει¹⁸ ὀργῆς ὡς καὶ οἱ
λοιποί·

τοῖς παραπτώμασιν καὶ ταῖς ἁμαρτίαις – When a dative does not refer to a person, it generally
has a referential meaning ("concerning").¹⁹ The repetition of the article may give equal and distinct weight to each term. But the second may be required by the possessive pronoun, if it is
original (see below). Of course, an article may have more than one function. παράπτωμα
evokes *making a false step, tripping up*. The substantive plays off the metaphor of life as journey (περιπατέω—v. 2; 4:1). ἁμαρτία may signify a *departure from a divine standard*
(BDAG), but more often describes willful rebellion against God. The terms move from particular to general. Cod.Vat reads ἐπιθυμίαις probably in anticipation of v. 3.

ποτε περιεπατήσατε – The aorist probably conveys perfective aspect. It is an external presenta-
tion of the action or state conveying *remoteness* at the semantic level.²⁰ with the adverb ποτε,
there is a distance between this way of life and the present state of being of the readers (hearers).
Contextually, Paul is referring to the past.

τῶν αἰώνων – may have a temporal ("age") or demonic deific referent ("Aeon"). The highest god in
Hellenism came to be known as *Aeon*. Some Gnostics used the term to identify a divine emana-
tion. Pauline use suggests the former (1:21!; see also 2 Cor 4:4; 1 Cor 2:6, 8).

τὸν ἄρχοντα τῆς ἐξουσίας – ἐξουσίας may be an objective genitive—"metonymy for the sphere
("domain") in which authority is exercised": "the one who rules with authority."²¹ Yet Paul may
also describe two powers: A Ruler and an Authority over the air. This might refer to Satan and
his collective demonic agency in the world. Like Revelation (chs. 12–13), we may have an unholy counterpart to the Son and Holy Spirit.²²

ἐν οἷς – the pronoun may be masculine or neuter, creating an ambiguity. On the one hand, the preposition ἐν may convey association ("among whom"), with the antecedent being the "sons of disobedience." On the other, it may have a locative sense, referring back to τοῖς παραπτώμασιν

---

occurrence. Yet demons would steal *into* the body through the orifices, sometimes, it was thought, consuming the vic-
tim's vital substance leading to death. Of course, these two senses may be complementary since the dative may convey
more than one meaning. Evil eventually works itself out into the world.

¹⁵ The participle may relate the result of the previous clause.

¹⁶ Subjective Genitive (Larkin, *Ephesians*, 29).

¹⁷ A Byz reading has ἤμεν.

¹⁸ The dative conveys cause.

¹⁹ Larkin suggests sphere, although that syntax is largely limited to the prepositions ἐν or εἰς (*Ephesians*,
27). See the textual problem at Col 2:13.

²⁰ Campbell, *Aspect*, 37. This is less disputed than the perfect tense, yet some still refer to "aoristic" aspect.

²¹ Larkin, *Ephesians*, 28.

²² Leland Ryken sees hints of the unholy Trinity here (*The Devotional Poetry of Donne, Herbert, and Milton*
[Wheaton, IL: Crossway, 2014], 23).

at v. 1. But the former is more likely because of proximity (so ESV).

ἡμεῖς – The original hands of Cod.Alex, Cod.Bezea, and other mss read ὑμεῖς in agreement with v. 1, if that reading is secure (see above). But the second, uncontested occurrence of "we" in the same sentence makes our reading more likely. Paul appears to be claiming that both Jews (himself being a representative) and Gentiles were oppressed by Satan's dominion. The pronoun is emphatic, emphasizing the inclusive subject.

ἐπιθυμίαις τῆς σαρκός and τὰ θελήματα τῆς σαρκός may be subjective genitives: "flesh *which causes* lust," "flesh *which causes* desires," as Larkin suggests, although the objective and therefore plenary make sense too: "lust" and "desire for flesh."[23] σάρξ may refer to the *outward side of life*, which often leads to pride (6:6; 1 Cor 1:26; 2 Cor 11:18).

διάνοια often translates "heart" (לֵב, לְבָב) in the LXX / OG. The plural suggests impulses or movements of desire (see Num 15:39).

ἤμεθα – The **imperfect tense** invites an imperfective viewpoint on a past action or, in this case, a state. The tense occurs more often in narrative, but Paul wants to emphasize the chronic enslavement.[24]

φύσει ὀργῆς may convey a **genitive of destination**. In this case, the word "destined" may be added to the translation: "children destined for wrath."[25]

2:4–7—NOW

⁴ ὁ[26] δὲ θεὸς πλούσιος ὢν ἐν ἐλέει,[27] διὰ[28] τὴν πολλὴν ἀγάπην[29] αὐτοῦ[30] ἣν ἠγάπησεν[31] ἡμᾶς, ⁵ καὶ ὄντας ἡμᾶς νεκροὺς τοῖς παραπτώμασιν[32] συνεζωοποίησεν[33] τῷ Χριστῷ— χάριτι[34]

---

[23] *Ephesians*, 29. The nouns ἐπιθυμία and θέλημα easily convert to verbs: ἐπιθυμέω and θέλω, respectively.

[24] In narrative, the imperfect tense-form often relates supplemental information, putting "flesh on the skeleton" from the aorist tense forms. It is "offline" information (Campbell, *Aspect*, 44).

[25] See Rom 8:36; Wallace, *Greek Grammar*, 100–101.

[26] The article identifies the one true God.

[27] ἐν ἐλέει is a Dative of Reference.

[28] The sense is causal with the accusative.

[29] διά...ἀγάπην is causal with the accusative.

[30] Omitted in P[46], the original hand of Cod.Bezae, Augustine, and others. The sense is little affected. If original, a Subjective Genitive is intended (Larkin, *Ephesians*, 30).

[31] The repetition of the root adds emphasis (Eadie, *Commentary*, 144). There is a surprising diversity of readings here. P[46] reads ἠλέησεν. The form occurs at Phil 2:7. The original hand of Cod.Bezae, ταῖς ἁμαρτίαις; later codices, τῇ ἁμαρτίᾳ or τοῖς παραπτώμασιν καὶ ταῖς ἁμαρτίαις; Cod.Vat, ἐν τοῖς παραπτώμασιν καὶ ταῖς ἐπιθυμίαις (see 2:1). Our text follows the redundant style of the letter, which may have given rise to the other readings. It is supported, in part, by Cod.Sinai and MT. The paranomasis adds emphasis (Larkin, *Ephesians*, 30).

[32] P[46] reads instead σώμασιν, "bodies." If original, the sense is sphere.

[33] P[46], Cod.Vat, and a few other mss read ἐν. The sense is little affected.

[34] The dative conveys means.

ἐστε σεσῳσμένοι[35]— ⁶ καὶ συνήγειρεν καὶ συνεκάθισεν ἐν τοῖς ἐπουρανίοις ἐν Χριστῷ
Ἰησοῦ, ⁷ ἵνα ἐνδείξηται ἐν τοῖς αἰῶσιν τοῖς ἐπερχομένοις τὸ[36] ὑπερβάλλον[37] πλοῦτος[38] τῆς
χάριτος[39] αὐτοῦ ἐν χρηστότητι ἐφ' ἡμᾶς ἐν Χριστῷ Ἰησοῦ.

δέ – As we noted, δέ cleaves the subunits. This subunit is further delimited by the repetition of the
   cognates πλούσιος and πλοῦτος.

ἐστε σεσῳσμένοι – This is a **perfect periphrastic construction**: "An anarthrous participle can be
   used with a verb of being (such as εἰμί or ὑπάρχω) to form a finite verbal idea. (If the participle
   was arthrous, it would necessarily function like an adjective.) This participle is called periphrastic because it is a *round-about* way of saying what could be expressed by a single verb."[40] It is
   nearly the equivalent of a finite verb in the perfect tense form. In some cases, this was probably
   done for simplicity: the perfect middle/passive participle is fairly easy to construct. The circumlocution may also emphasize stativity, the enduring results of a completed action.[41] The state-of-
   being verb and perfect tense form of the participle complement one another.

2:8–10—THE CAUSE OF SALVATION

⁸ τῇ γὰρ χάριτί ἐστε σεσῳσμένοι[42] διὰ τῆς πίστεως· καὶ τοῦτο οὐκ ἐξ[43] ὑμῶν, θεοῦ[44] τὸ
δῶρον· ⁹ οὐκ ἐξ ἔργων, ἵνα μή τις καυχήσηται.[45] ¹⁰ αὐτοῦ[46] γάρ ἐσμεν ποίημα, κτισθέντες ἐν
Χριστῷ Ἰησοῦ[47] ἐπὶ[48] ἔργοις ἀγαθοῖς οἷς[49] προητοίμασεν ὁ θεὸς ἵνα ἐν αὐτοῖς[50]
περιπατήσωμεν.

τῇ γὰρ χάριτί ἐστε σεσῳσμένοι – This subunit beginning with this statement unpacks the nearly
   identical periphrastic claim in v. 5 (χάριτί ἐστε σεσῳσμένοι). Paul employs the rhetorical device
   anadiplosis (ἀναδίπλωσις "redoubling") where an element (often unimportant or parenthetical)
   in one sentence is repeated in the following sentence, but with a change or extension of the sense,

---

[35] The perfect emphasizes the resulting state.

[36] Byz mss read τόν.

[37] Byz mss read ὑπερβάλλοντα.

[38] Byz mss read πλοῦτον.

[39] Larkin suggests the genitive is epexegetical (*Ephesians*, 32).

[40] Wallace, *Greek Grammar*, 647.

[41] Hoehner, *Ephesians*, 341. Technically, the construction has imperfective and stative aspect!

[42] See v. 5.

[43] The preposition conveys source or is possibly causal.

[44] A Genitive of Source (Larkin, *Ephesians*, 33). The fronting of the genitive is emphatic.

[45] An aorist middle subjunctive. The act of boasting is self-involving.

[46] A Genitive of Possession. Fronted for emphasis.

[47] In Christ or instrumentally "through" or "by" (Talbert, *Ephesians and Colossian*, 69).

[48] Larkin suggests the preposition conveys purpose (*Ephesians*, 34), yet Wallace does not list this category.

[49] οἷς conveys a Dative of Reference.

[50] ἐν αὐτοῖς conveys a Dative of Means.

now in v.8 unpacked. This unpacking is signaled by the particle γὰρ and the article τῇ which is **anaphoric** (ἀναφέρω "bring up," previous reference). When an article is pointing backward to an earlier occurrence, the translation "this" is acceptable: "For by *this* grace."

γάρ – This is the first occurrence of γὰρ in the letter. The postpositive conjunction functions to strengthen a preceding proposition.[51]

τῇ ... χάριτι – The dative χάριτι may convey the means, instrument, or manner of an action. In this case, it is God's kind disposition. χάρις signifies God's beneficent disposition towards his people. Paul distances the language from the cultural reciprocity system where "grace" was often deserved.[52] God extended grace because he loved us.

ἐστε σεσῳσμένοι – This is a periphrastic construction. For Paul, the agency of salvation is overdetermined: ἐστε σεσῳσμένοι is probably a divine passive. This periphrastic construction may entail an **intensive perfect**, which highlights the results of an action. Wallace explains,

> The average student learning NT Greek typically knows Greek grammar better than English grammar after a couple of years of study. Consequently, the aspect of the Greek perfect is sometimes imported into the English perfect. That is, there is a tendency to see the English perfect as placing an emphasis on existing results—a notion foreign to English grammar. As Moule notes, "the Greek tense is concerned with *result*, while the English tense is concerned solely with the absence . . . of an *interval*." One ought to be careful when translating the perfect into English to resist the temptation to translate it as an English perfect at all times. When so translated, the Greek perfect should be extensive [focusing on the completed action], not intensive.
>
> Along these lines, it should be noted that as many faults as the KJV has, it frequently has a superior rendering of the Greek perfect over many modern translations. (Recall that the KJV was produced during the golden age of English, during Shakespeare's era.) For example, in Eph 2:8 the KJV reads "for by grace are ye saved," while many modern translations (e.g., RSV, NASB) have "for by grace you have been saved." The perfect periphrastic construction is most likely intensive, however. The KJV translators, though not having nearly as good a grasp on Greek as modern translators, seem to have had a better grasp on English. They apparently recognized that to translate Eph 2:8 with an English perfect would say nothing about the state resulting from the act of being saved.[53]

Wallace suggests, following the KJV, that we translate intensive perfects with the English present. We are therefore not surprised by the NET's translation: "For by grace you are saved through faith." However, according to one authority, the **English present perfect** (auxiliary

---

[51] Black, *Conjunctions*, 265.

[52] Talbert, *Ephesians*, 67.

[53] *Greek Grammar*, 575, references omitted.

verb have/has + past participle) "captures the idea that there is some *current relevance* to the past action, or that as of this time, one *has had the experience* of doing something."[54] This definition seems to approximate results.

σεσωσμένοι – Interestingly, σῴζω occurs in Ephesians only in this context (2:5, 8); its cognates σωτήρ "savior" and σωτήριος "bring salvation" occur in 5:23 and 6:17, respectively. Regardless of what English tense is used for σῴζω here (see the above discussion), the context suggests a past deliverance causing a present state of beatitude in Christ.[55] For Paul, the agency of salvation is overdetermined: ἐστε σεσωσμένοι is probably a divine passive. The dative χάριτί may convey the means, instrument, or manner of an action. In this case, it is God's kind disposition.

καὶ τοῦτο is much discussed. At least since **Jerome** and **Chrysostom**, the antecedent of the demonstrative pronoun τοῦτο has been understood to be πίστεως (πίστις). This is also a popular interpretation among Reformed interpreters. The proximate implication of οὗτος (in contrast to ἐκεῖνος) might suggest this—the pronoun generally points to something or someone close at hand. Yet the genders do not correlate. It could also point ahead to a **postcedent**—δῶρον that is neuter.[56] But the simplest reading is a **clausal antecedent**—the pronoun refers to Τῇ γὰρ χάριτί ἐστε σεσωσμένοι διὰ [τῆς] πίστεως.[57] (We often conceptualize antecedents as single words, but this is not always the case.)

διὰ πίστεως – The preposition διά often conveys secondary agency.[58] If this refers to the faith of the Ephesians, then we have divine agency and human responsibility as part of the puzzle, although the former is dominant. πίστις includes loyalty.[59]

We have the variant here with the addition of the article τῆς to form διὰ τῆς πίστεως "through the faith," which occurs in Cod.Alex and becomes part of **the Majority Text** (MT). The article typically identifies a specific expression of a class. On the one hand, a scribe may have wanted the claim to refer to "the Faith"—perhaps a confession: Τὸ δὲ πνεῦμα ῥητῶς λέγει ὅτι ἐν ὑστέροις καιροῖς ἀποστήσονταί τινες τῆς πίστεως προσέχοντες πνεύμασιν πλάνοις καὶ διδασκαλίαις δαιμονίων (1 Tim 4:1).[60] If so, one may argue against the originality of the variant, sensing a theological bias. On the other, Paul may refer to "the faith" or "faithfulness of Jesus Christ," as the next occurrence of πίστις, which is also arthrous and the object of the preposition διά, suggests: ἐν ᾧ ἔχομεν τὴν παρρησίαν καὶ προσαγωγὴν ἐν πεποιθήσει διὰ τῆς

---

[54] Anne Stilman, *Grammatically Correct:* The Essential Guide to Spelling, Style, Usage, Grammar, and Punctuation, 2nd ed. (Cincinnati, OH: Writer's Digest Books, 2010), 242, emphasis hers.

[55] Note the aorist tense forms: περιεπατήσατε, ἀνεστράφημέν, ἠγάπησεν, συνεζωοποίησεν, συνήγειρεν, and συνεκάθισεν. There is also the past state described with ἤμεθα and present participles.

[56] Some read the pronoun as an adverb "and indeed" (see Eadie, *Ephesians,* 155).

[57] Wallace, *Greek Grammar,* 333–34; Larkin, *Ephesians,* 33. We find similar constructions in Latin, Greek's sister language.

[58] Eadie, *Commentary,* 153.

[59] Talbert, *Ephesians,* 67.

[60] See also 1 Tim 1:2; 3:9; 4:6; 5:8; 6:10, 12, 21. The expression is also common in the other Pastoral Letters.

πίστεως αὐτοῦ (3:12).[61] The KJV reads: "In whom we have boldness and access with confidence by the faith of him." For a while, modern translations departed from this reading, probably for the sake of consistency, reading the Genitive as Objective (NAS, ESV). But there seems to be a movement to return: "in whom we have boldness and confident access to God because of Christ's faithfulness" (NET).[62] Perhaps early copyists omitted the article at 2:8 because they did not recognize its anticipatory function. But if the article is original, it is most likely anaphoric, referring back to τὴν καθ᾽ ὑμᾶς πίστιν, which is especially emphatic (1:15).

αὐτοῦ is fronted for emphasis, with the antecedent being God.

ἐπὶ ἔργοις ἀγαθοῖς – The preposition ἐπί with the dative may convey a spatial ("upon") or causal ("on the basis of") sense. The former makes sense if Paul intends the good works of God's salvation, raising and glorifying Christ leading to new creation; the latter, a more plausible reading, our *raison d'être*. The language evokes the Mosaic Law: "If you walk (תֵּלֵכוּ) in my statutes and observe my commandments (מִצְוֹתַי) and do them, then I will give you your rains in their season…" (Lev 26:3–4 ESV).

ἐν αὐτοῖς – The preposition ἐν may convey a spatial ("in") or instrumental ("by") sense.

ACTIVITIES & QUESTIONS

1. How many verbs in this unit have the prefixed preposition σύν? What are the soteriological (salvific) implications?

2. With software or a concordance, review all the occurrences of πίστις in Ephesians. Try to build up the semantic range of the word in the letter—what does it mean in the broadest sense? Take an especially careful look at 4:13. Then take a position on the variant at v. 8—διὰ [τῆς] πίστεως. Is Paul referring to our faith or the faith(fullness) of Jesus Christ? What are the theological implications of the latter reading?

3. How might the occurrence of περιπατέω at v. 2 inform the meaning of its repetition at v. 10?

---

[61] We run into the same ambiguity at 3:17.
[62] See also 4:13.

WEEK 5—EPH 2:11–22

Key Terms: subject-complement double nominative construction, metonymy, genitive of separation, litotes, Fenton John Anthony Hort

Vocabulary

ἄθεος, ον – without God	μνημονεύω – I remember, mention
ἀκροβυστία – uncircumcision, foreskin	νυνί – now
ἀκρογωνιαῖος, α, ον – cornerstone, capstone	ξένος, η, ον – strange
ἀμφότεροι, αι, α – both	οἰκοδομή, ῆς, ἡ – building, structure
ἀπαλλοτριόω – I estrange, alienate	οἰκεῖος, ον – member of a household
ἀποκαταλλάσσω – I reconcile	πάροικος, ον – foreigner
αὔξω, αὐξάνω – I grow	πολιτεία, ας, ἡ – citizenship
δόγμα, ατος, τό – rule	ποτέ – formerly
ἐποικοδομέω – I build on	προσαγωγή, ῆς, ἡ – entrance
ἔχθρα, ας, ἡ – enmity	χειροποίητος, ον – made by human hands
θεμέλιος, ου, ὁ – foundation	σταυρός, οῦ, ὁ – cross
καταργέω – I abolish	συμπολίτης, ου, ὁ – fellow-citizen
κατοικητήριον, ου, τό – dwelling	συναρμολογέω – I be joined together
κτίζω – I create	συνοικοδομέω – I build together
μακράν – far away	φραγμός, οῦ, ὁ – wall
μεσότοιχον, ου, τό – dividing wall	

Cutting at the Joints: διό marks the transition to a new unit. The inferential particle introduces exhortation after a teaching section elsewhere.[1] The imperative μνημονεύετε is premature according to structural analyses that separate the "is" from the "ought" in Ephesians. Otherwise, the imperatives occur in the second half of the book.

Like the previous unit, Paul offers a before (vv. 11–12) and after picture, cleaved by νυνὶ δὲ (v. 13). The second subunit (vv. 13–18) is delimited by the *inclusio*: **you who . . . far off**. Verse 18 anticipates the final subunit, serving as a latch.

Ἄρα οὖν (v. 19), if original (see below), would transition to a new subunit. It is especially emphatic: Ἄρα expressing inference; οὖν, transition.[2]

The focus also shifts from the Father to the Son and Spirit.

---

[1] See 3:13; 4:25; Larkin, *Ephesians*, 36.
[2] Larkin, *Ephesians*, 43.

2:11–22—ONE IN CHRIST

The unit echoes the previous (2:1–10), rehearsing the negative plight of the readers before Christ and their salvation, but highlights the horizontal implications (justice, *communitas*). God loves us, but also our enemies, and has united both groups in Christ into one family (temple, people). Also echoing the Greeting (1:2), we saw grace (vv. 5, 8) and now peace (vv. 14, 15).

2:11–12—THEN

> [11] Διὸ μνημονεύετε ὅτι³ ποτὲ ὑμεῖς⁴ τὰ ἔθνη⁵ ἐν σαρκί, οἱ λεγόμενοι ἀκροβυστία ὑπὸ τῆς λεγομένης περιτομῆς ἐν σαρκὶ χειροποιήτου, [12] ὅτι⁶ ἦτε⁷ τῷ καιρῷ ἐκείνῳ χωρὶς Χριστοῦ, ἀπηλλοτριωμένοι τῆς πολιτείας τοῦ Ἰσραὴλ καὶ ξένοι⁸ τῶν διαθηκῶν τῆς ἐπαγγελίας, ἐλπίδα μὴ ἔχοντες καὶ ἄθεοι ἐν τῷ κόσμῳ.

Διό – Two later codices read instread Διὰ τοῦτο thus recapitulating 1:15. Although I favor the shorter, earlier reading, the variant helpfully reminds us of the distance from the last inferential conjunction. Paul is assuming the discussion at least from 1:20.

μνημονεύετε (μνημονεύω) – The verb may be read as an indicative, but context suggests the imperative. Paul uses the root in the context of prayer (1:16). The verb signifies memory, but also mindfulness (μνήμων "mindful"). The present tense encodes imperfective aspect, which often depicts general commands. The *Aktionsart* is progressive: Paul is exhorting the Ephesians to be continually aware of this reality as a way of renewing their mind.

ποτὲ ὑμεῖς – This opening clause that the readers are to remember has an implied state of being verb: "Therefore, remember that you *were* formerly...."

οἱ λεγόμενοι ἀκροβυστία – Why is ἀκροβυστία in the nominative case? οἱ λεγόμενοι ἀκροβυστία may be a complement in a **subject-complement double nominative construction**. According to Martin Culy, this is common with the verb καλέω.⁹ For example, in the active voice I say, "I call you Mary." When such a clause is "passivized"—turned into the passive voice—the object ("you") and complement ("Mary") take the nominative case form ("You are called Mary"). In the passive voice, the direct object becomes the subject. In this case, "you were called foreskin." Although the subject is not explicit, it is assumed.

---

³ ὅτι introduces indirect discourse.

⁴ ποτὲ makes a conjugated verb unnecessary. The tense is made explicit with ἦτε in the following clause (v. 12). Byz mss read ὑμεῖς ποτὲ. ὑμεῖς is emphatic with an implied verb as we saw at 2:1.

⁵ ἔθνη is appositional to ὑμεῖς.

⁶ The ὅτι introduces indirect discourse, and is appositional to the ὅτι at v. 11 (Larkin, *Ephesians*, 37).

⁷ Byz mss read ἐν.

⁸ ὁ ξένος is the opposite of πολίτης or "citizen" (Philo, *Post.* 109; Josephus, *Ant.* 11.159; *Vita* 372).

⁹ "Double Case Constructions in Koine Greek," *JGRChJ* 6 (2009): 82–106, esp. 85. But he does not list this verse as an example.

ἀκροβυστία – The noun, probably derived from ἀκροποσθία ("tip of foreskin"), often functions as the object of ἔχω, describing "someone who has a foreskin" (Gen 34:14; Acts 11:3). The slur is **metonymy** (μετωνυμία, "a change of name") for Nations (Gentiles). The contemporary work *Rhetorica ad Herennium* describes metonymy as "the figure which draws from an object closely akin or associated an expression suggesting the object meant, but not called by its own name." Associating someone with a private part is a common insult in English. Its force is reductionism, especially in the case of people who are created in God's image.

περιτομῆς – The same may be said for περιτομή (περιτέμνω). The prefixed preposition περί may describe a circular motion—"around." The stem is derived from the verb τέμνω "to cut." Although we should avoid the fallacy of reading every prefixed verb literally, in this case it seems warranted: περιτομή graphically describes someone who has been cut around the penis.

On the one hand, an ἀκροβυστία and περιτομή could not be more different—the foreskin and the absence of foreskin, respectively. On the other, they were originally attached before God separated the parts for the sake of covenant. Now, in the New Covenant, they may be reunited.

χειροποιήτου (χειροποίητος) – The two-termination, predicate verbal adjective usually describes buildings, specifically temples (Mark 14:58; Acts 7:48; Philo, *Mos.* 2.88; *Sib. Or.* 14.62). The stem echoes ποίημα, providing a latching effect, implying a contrast between divine and human agency (see 2:10).

ἀπηλλοτριωμένοι (ἀπαλλοτριόω, "estrange," "alienate") – the perfect tense allows a stative *Aktionsart*. The Nations (peoples, Gentiles) exist alienated from God and God's people.[10]

τῆς πολιτείας is a **genitive of separation**—"the genitive is used to indicate the point of departure."[11] We may add "(away) from" for the sense. For this reason, the case is used with the preposition ἐκ (before vowels ἐξ).

πολιτεία refers to a sociopolitical unit or body of citizens.[12]

τοῦ Ἰσραήλ is an indeclinable transliteration of the Hebrew יִשְׂרָאֵל. Paul uses the article to refer to God's people who bear the patriarch's name (Rom 9:6; 10:21; 11:2; contrast with Phil 3:5).

The parallelism suggests Christ was already united to Israel as their representative head.

2:13–17—NOW

The unit is delimited by Paul's exegesis of Isaiah, with the lemmas preceding the citation. The adverb and conjunction νυνὶ δέ offers a dramatic reversal (see 2:4).

---

[10] Third Macc 1:3 uses some of the vocabulary of this unit.

[11] Wallace, *Greek Grammar*, 107. In older grammars, this syntax was associated with the ablative case. Occasionally, one finds the description "Ablative Genitive."

[12] BDAG s.v. πολιτεία.

¹³ νυνὶ δὲ ἐν¹³ Χριστῷ Ἰησοῦ ὑμεῖς οἵ ποτε ὄντες¹⁴ **μακρὰν** ἐγενήθητε ἐγγὺς¹⁵ ἐν¹⁶ τῷ
αἵματι τοῦ Χριστοῦ.¹⁷ **¹⁴** αὐτὸς γάρ ἐστιν ἡ **εἰρήνη** ἡμῶν, ὁ ποιήσας τὰ ἀμφότερα ἒν¹⁸ καὶ τὸ
μεσότοιχον τοῦ φραγμοῦ λύσας, τὴν ἔχθραν ἐν τῇ σαρκὶ αὐτοῦ, **¹⁵** τὸν νόμον τῶν ἐντολῶν ἐν
δόγμασιν¹⁹ καταργήσας, ἵνα τοὺς δύο κτίσῃ ἐν αὐτῷ²⁰ εἰς ἕνα [καινὸν]²¹ ἄνθρωπον ποιῶν
εἰρήνην, **¹⁶** καὶ ἀποκαταλλάξῃ τοὺς ἀμφοτέρους ἐν ἑνὶ σώματι τῷ θεῷ διὰ τοῦ σταυροῦ,
ἀποκτείνας τὴν ἔχθραν ἐν αὐτῷ.²² **¹⁷ καὶ ἐλθὼν εὐηγγελίσατο εἰρήνην ὑμῖν τοῖς**
μακρὰν καὶ εἰρήνην²³ τοῖς ἐγγύς· [Isa 52:7; 57:19]

ἐν τῷ αἵματι τοῦ Χριστοῦ – In the LXX, we find the phrase τὸ αἷμα τῆς περιτομῆς (Exod 4:25,
26). Perhaps Jesus's αἷμα fulfills this practice.

εἰρήνη (שָׁלוֹם) describes *a communal harmony of mutual wellbeing*. It begins by allowing Christ to
reign in our hearts (Col 2:15).

ὑμεῖς is again emphatic (2:11). So is Αὐτός.

τὸ μεσότοιχον is a rare noun referring to a "dividing wall," possibly alluding to the four and half
foot balustrade in the Second Temple, which separated Jews and Gentiles.²⁴

τοῦ φραγμοῦ – Interpreters vary in their assessment: Purpose (Wallace), attributed, or epexegetical
(Larkin).²⁵

ποιῶν εἰρήνην – The switch to the present imperfective participle conveys ongoing peacemaking.

διὰ τοῦ σταυροῦ – another example of **metonymy**. It is probably not the wood artifact, but what
the Father and Son accomplished on the cross that matters.

Paul may offer a second biblical citation—a *gezerah sheva* from Isaiah with the element of pro-
claiming the gospel from 52:7 and the scope from 57:19. However, without a citation formula,
the earlier texts function elusively.

---

[13] The ἐν conveys a Dative of Sphere.

[14] In this case, the present tense form of the participle cannot refer to action simultaneous with the conjugated
verb it modifies. The vantage point is imperfective on a previous state of being.

[15] Byz mss read ἐγγὺς ἐγενήθητε.

[16] ἐν conveys an Instrumental Dative. The agent of the passive voice is God the Father.

[17] τοῦ Χριστοῦ is omitted in P⁴⁶ and Cod.Vat.

[18] ἒν functions as a complement in an object-complement Double Accusative construction.

[19] ἐν δόγμασιν is omitted in P⁴⁶ and a few Latin mss.

[20] The corrector of Cod.Sin, Cod.Bezae, and Byz read ἑαυτῷ.

[21] P⁴⁶ and two later mss read κοινόν ("one common human being"); another late codex, καὶ μόνον ("one and
only human being"). Both are interesting variants yet weakly attested.

[22] Two later codices read ἑαυτῷ instead of ἐν αὐτῷ. Otherwise, the antecedent could be the cross (Larkin,
Ephesians, 42).

[23] Omitted in Byz. The variant is not significant because the sense would be presumed in the ellipsis.

[24] Paul does not us ἀλλογενής, the term on the temple warning inscription.

[25] *Greek Grammar*, 100; *Ephesians*, 40.

2:18–22—RESULT OF CHRIST'S PEACE

This unit is delimited by *inclusio*: ἐν ἑνὶ πνεύματι. Remember that reference to "spiritual blessing" (εὐλογία πνευματικῇ) and the Holy Spirit wrapped the opening *berakah* (1:3, 13).

> **18** ὅτι[26] δι᾽ αὐτοῦ ἔχομεν τὴν προσαγωγὴν οἱ ἀμφότεροι ἐν ἑνὶ πνεύματι πρὸς τὸν πατέρα. **19** Ἄρα οὖν οὐκέτι ἐστὲ ξένοι καὶ πάροικοι[27] ἀλλὰ ἐστὲ[28] συμπολῖται τῶν ἁγίων καὶ οἰκεῖοι τοῦ θεοῦ, **20** ἐποικοδομηθέντες ἐπὶ τῷ **θεμελίῳ** τῶν ἀποστόλων καὶ προφητῶν, ὄντος **ἀκρογωνιαίου**[29] αὐτοῦ Χριστοῦ Ἰησοῦ[30], **21** ἐν ᾧ πᾶσα οἰκοδομὴ[31] συναρμολογουμένη[32] αὔξει εἰς ναὸν ἅγιον ἐν κυρίῳ, **22** ἐν ᾧ καὶ ὑμεῖς συνοικοδομεῖσθε[33] εἰς κατοικητήριον τοῦ θεοῦ[34] ἐν πνεύματι. [Isa 28:16]

προσαγωγή – BDAG offers two different glosses for προσαγωγή: a way of approach and access. Xenophon significantly uses the word to describe access to Cyrus for an audience, who is the earthly foil of the Servant in Isaiah:

> "I see also," he went on, "still another absurd feature in all this: while my affection for you is, as you know, what it naturally ought to be, of these who stand about here I know few or none; and yet all these have made up their minds that if they can get ahead of you in crowding in, they will obtain what they wish from me before you can. Now what I expected all such to do, if any one wanted anything from me, was to get into favour with you as my friends and ask you for an introduction (προσαγωγή)." (*Cyr.* 7.5.45)[35]

Ἄρα οὖν – The second inferential particle is omitted in P[46] and a few later codices.[36] Perhaps it was omitted because of the seeming redundancy or, more likely, homoioarcton: οὖν οὐκέτι (review week 3). Yet we find the combination throughout the *corpus Paulinum* (Rom 5:18; 7:3, 25; 8:12; 9:16, 18; 14:19; Gal 6:10; 1 Thess 5:6; 2 Thess 2:15). It seems less plausible for the article to be added. So the older, longer reading is preferred! If we accept the reading, *this is the strongest conclusion to an argument up to this point in the letter*. It suggests a rhetorical situa-

---

[26] ὅτι functions causally.

[27] Either ξένοι or πάροικοι may translate the Hebrew *gēr* ("immigrant" or "sojourner").

[28] Omitted in the first corrector of Cod.Bezae and Byz mss. Such ellipsis is common after ἀλλά. It is difficult to understand why a scribe would add the unnecessary verb.

[29] The original hand of Cod.Bezae and a few other mss read λίθου. The variant only makes explicit what is at least implicit in ἀκρογωνιαίου.

[30] Byz mss read Ἰησοῦ χριστοῦ.

[31] The first corrector of Cod.Sinai, Cod.Alex, and a few other later mss add an article (ἡ) to the substantive.

[32] The architectural imagery is the squaring of stones to fit them into a building (Larkin, *Ephesians*, 46).

[33] Present passive (divine). The verb signifies the building up or constructing of various parts.

[34] Cod.Vat reads χριστοῦ.

[35] The translation is from Xenophon, *Cyropaedia*, 2 vols. (Cambridge: Harvard University Press, 1994), 2:279.

[36] The variant is labelled "vid" in NA[28], which means there is some ambiguity about the reading, but seems to be confirmed by Comfort and Barrett, *The Text of The Earliest New Testament*, 306.

tion of conflict between Jews and Gentiles. Is the conflict with Jews inside or outside the church? The context suggests the former: Paul has opposed a Jewish group that required Gentile believers to be circumcised for salvation (Gal, 2 Cor, Phil).

πάροικος is a sad word, referring to someone who lives in a place that is not his or her home.

οὐκέτι ἐστὲ ξένοι καὶ πάροικοι ἀλλὰ ἐστὲ συμπολῖται... – Paul employs the rhetorical device **litotes**—asserting the negative to emphasize the positive. This is often signaled by the strong adversative conjunction ἀλλά as found here. The point is not to ignore the negative, but to emphasize the positive—the full inclusion of Gentiles into God's people.

οἰκεῖος, from οἶκος, describes members of a household.

τῶν ἀποστόλων καὶ προφητῶν – Technically, this is not an example of the Granville Sharp Rule because the nouns are plural.[37] Yet this plural personal construction suggests distinct yet united groups.[38] Traditionally, the prophets have been understood as the OT writers (Marius Victorinus, Calvin), making the apostles and prophets two different groups. It is tempting to hear a reformulation of the contemporary expression "Torah and Prophets." But Paul probably refers to contemporary prophets serving the church (3:5; 4:11; 1 Cor 12:28–29). Early Christian prophets believed the spirit of prophecy had been renewed in the new age inaugurated by Christ (see Acts 13:1–3; 1 Cor 14; Matt 7:15–20; *Did.* 11–13). Perhaps the apostle refers to both biblical and contemporary prophets. The apostles signify the Twelve (1 Cor 15:5) or the 120–500 (1 Cor 15:6; Acts 1:6–15). If the former are intended, the relationship with Prophets is tighter with Pentecost in the background. **Fenton John Anthony Hort** (1828–1892) suggests reading καὶ προφητῶν in apposition with ἀποστόλων—"apostles—namely, prophets." Today, we call this an epexegetical καί. This reading seems forced.[39]

ἀκρογωνιαῖος – This term may refer to a "cornerstone," befitting the immediate context, but also a "capstone," which matches the idea of Jesus as head (κεφαλή) of the Church (see BDAG). If Paul alludes to Isa 28:16, which is probable, the former is more likely because פִּנָּה more naturally refers to a "corner." We find an explicit citation of Isa 28:16 in 1 Pet 2:6.

ναὸν ἅγιον – A building within the larger temple complex. With the adjective, we have a reference to a new "Holy of Holies." The absence of an article emphasizes the quality of holiness. This contextualizes the Trinitarian language of the subunit.

ἐποικοδομηθέντες ... συνοικοδομεῖσθε – Paul vacillates between two prefixes to describe the construction of the temple: ἐποικοδομέω ("to build on") and συνοικοδομέω ("to build with").[40]

---

[37] Review week 2 and see Wallace, *Greek Grammar*, 270–90.

[38] Larkin, *Ephesians*, 44.

[39] C. F. D. Moule, *An Idiom Book of New Testament Greek* (Cambridge: Cambridge University Press, 1953), 110.

[40] BDAG obscures the meaning of συνοικοδομέω: see 1 Esdr 5:65 and the extensive use of the *sun* prefix in a previous unit (2:1–6).

ACTIVITIES & QUESTIONS

1. With software or a concordance, look up every occurrence of ἀπόστολος and προφήτης in Paul's letters; then, considering the immediate context, suggest what the terms refer to at v. 20 and their relationship to one another—same, overlapping, or distinct.

2. Calvin notes: "Put all these things together, and you will frame the following syllogism: If the Jews wish to enjoy peace with God, they must have Christ as their Mediator. But Christ will not be their peace in any other way than by making them one body with the Gentiles. Therefore, unless the Jews admit the Gentiles to fellowship with them, they have no friendship with God."[41] How might we teach this passage today?

3. Reword Calvin's syllogism according to your convictions. For example, during the civil rights movement, one might have written: "If *white Christians* wish to enjoy peace with God, they must have Christ as their Mediator. But Christ will not be their peace in any other way than by making them one body with *African American Christians*. Therefore, unless *the white Christians* admit *the African American Christian* to fellowship with them, they have no friendship with God."

---

[41] *The Epistles of Paul to the Galatians and Ephesians*, 236.

WEEK 6—EPH 3:1–13

Key Terms: digression, improper preposition, anacoluthon, *nominativus pendens*, immediate past/dramatic aorist, Philo, appositional infinitive, comparative as superlative, neologism

Vocabulary

ἀναγινώσκω – I read	νοέω – I understand
ἀνεξιχνίαστος, ον – fathomless, incomprehensible	οἰκονομία, ας, ἡ – stewardship, plan
ἀποκαλύπτω – I reveal	ὀλίγος, η, ον – few
ἀποκάλυψις, εως, ἡ – revelation	πεποίθησις, εως, ἡ – confidence
ἀποκρύπτω – I hide	πλοῦτος, ου, ὁ – wealth
γέ – even, indeed	πολυποίκιλος, ον – in varied forms
γνωρίζω – I make known	προγράφω – I write beforehand
δέσμιος, ου, ὁ – prisoner	πρόθεσις, εως, ἡ – purpose
διάκονος, ου, ὁ, ἡ – servant, minister, deacon	προσαγωγή, ῆς, ἡ – access
δωρεά, ᾶς, ἡ – gift	συγκληρονόμος, ον – coheir
ἐγκακέω – I become discouraged	συμμέτοχος, ον – participant
ἐλάχιστος, ίστη, ον – least	σύνεσις, εως, ἡ – insight
ἐνέργεια, ας, ἡ – working	σύσσωμος, ον – belonging to the same body
ἐπουράνιος, ον – heavenly	
κτίζω – I create	φωτίζω – I enlighten
μυστήριον, ου, τό – mystery	χάριν – because of (stands after its object)

Sharing personal circumstances often marks a transition to **the body**, although we are well into the letter. The unit also marks the beginning of Paul's intercessory prayer.

Cutting at the Joints: The unit is framed by *inclusio*—Paul's work on behalf (ὑπὲρ ὑμῶν) of the Gentiles (3:1, 13). The rhetorical marker Τούτου χάριν, rare in Paul's letters (3:14; Titus 1:5), links inferentially with the preceding unit.[1]

At v. 2, the apostle offers a **digression** (παρέκβασις), perhaps as a result of mentioning his imprisonment for preaching the gospel to Gentiles. Digressions were common in speeches, as Peter Perry notes, "Audiences would pay more attention to these passages because they require additional processing effort, they shape the ethos of author and audience, and they excite their emotions."[2]

---

[1] Lincoln, *Ephesians*, 172.
[2] *The Rhetoric of Digressions* (Tübingen: Mohr Siebeck, 2009), 242.

A rhetorically effective piece, according to the Aristotelian canon, establishes the credibility of the speaker (writer) through *ethos*, arouses the emotions of the audience (reader) through *pathos*, and grounds the claims in reality through logical consistency or *logos*. In this case, it clarifies the nature of the mystery, endearing Paul to his Gentile audience: ὑπὲρ ὑμῶν τῶν ἐθνῶν. They are full participants in God's dramatic plan to save creation. Apocalyptic elements emphasize the "mystery" of the gospel.

3:1–13—THE MYSTERY OF THE GOSPEL

3:1–7—The Grace of God

3.1 Τούτου χάριν[3] ἐγὼ Παῦλος ὁ δέσμιος τοῦ Χριστοῦ Ἰησοῦ[4] ὑπὲρ[5] ὑμῶν τῶν ἐθνῶν— **2** εἴ γε[6] ἠκούσατε τὴν οἰκονομίαν τῆς χάριτος τοῦ θεοῦ τῆς[7] δοθείσης[8] μοι εἰς ὑμᾶς· **3** [ὅτι][9] κατὰ ἀποκάλυψιν[10] ἐγνωρίσθη[11] μοι τὸ μυστήριον, καθὼς προέγραψα ἐν ὀλίγῳ, **4** πρὸς ὃ[12] δύνασθε ἀναγινώσκοντες[13] νοῆσαι τὴν σύνεσίν μου ἐν τῷ μυστηρίῳ τοῦ Χριστοῦ, **5** ὃ[14] ἑτέραις γενεαῖς οὐκ ἐγνωρίσθη τοῖς υἱοῖς τῶν ἀνθρώπων ὡς νῦν ἀπεκαλύφθη[15] τοῖς ἁγίοις ἀποστόλοις αὐτοῦ καὶ προφήταις ἐν πνεύματι,[16] **6** εἶναι τὰ ἔθνη συγκληρονόμα καὶ σύσσωμα καὶ συμμέτοχα τῆς ἐπαγγελίας[17] ἐν Χριστῷ Ἰησοῦ[18] διὰ τοῦ εὐαγγελίου, **7** οὗ

---

[3] The emphatic pronoun is a topic in a topic construction where the focal point of the unit is brought forward. The verb is not stated until v. 14!

[4] Ἰησοῦ has strong textual support (P[46], Cod.Vat, and Byz) although placed inside brackets in the NA[28]. See also v. 6 and 1:1. Otherwise, τοῦ Χριστοῦ might have a titular sense, "the Christ (Messiah)."

[5] The dative conveys advantage.

[6] Byz treats the two particles as one word (εἴγε). By way of qualification, Paul introduces an assumed condition (2 Cor 5:3; Gal 3:4; Eph 3:2; 4:21; Col 1:23). There is no sense of doubt.

[7] The article typically "bears an anaphoric force, pointing back to the substantive with which it has concord"—in this case, either οἰκονομία or χάρις (Wallace, *Greek Grammar*, 214). The latter is more probable because it is closer and is repeated with the participle at v. 7.

[8] The suffix -θείσης breaks the participle down into an aorist passive, genitive singular. The voice may be classified as a divine passive—God gave a specific οἰκονομία to Paul.

[9] Contrary to *SBLGNT*, I believe ὅτι was originally at the beginning of the verse, following Cod.Sinai and many Byz witnesses. The textual support marshaled above for "Jesus" (v. 1) omits ὅτι. If we follow this reading, a full stop is intended. But the short sentence does not comport with the style of the letter (Larkin, *Ephesians*, 51).

[10] Two later codices read a γάρ after ἀποκάλυψιν. The particle was probably intended to clarify the ambiguous syntax.

[11] Second hand of Cod.Bezae and Byz mss read ἐγνώρισέν.

[12] The antecedent of ὃ is μυστήριον.

[13] The participle is adverbial and conveys means (Wallace, *Greek Grammar*, 628).

[14] The antecedent of the neuter ὃ is μυστήριον.

[15] The adverb νῦν adds an interesting dimension to the aorist. In this case, the emphasis may be on the enduring result, like we often find with the perfect tense. Note the cognate repetition (ἀποκάλυψιν, v. 3).

[16] The dative is instrumental.

[17] Byz mss place αὐτοῦ after ἐπαγγελίας. The earlier, shorter, more difficult reading is preferred.

[18] Byz mss read τῷ χριστῷ.

ἐγενήθην[19] διάκονος κατὰ τὴν δωρεὰν τῆς χάριτος τοῦ θεοῦ τῆς δοθείσης[20] μοι κατὰ τὴν ἐνέργειαν τῆς δυνάμεως αὐτοῦ—

inclusio – This subunit is established by the *inclusio* τῆς χάριτος τοῦ θεοῦ τῆς δοθείσης μοι (3:2) // τῆς χάριτος τοῦ θεοῦ τῆς δοθείσης μοι (v. 7).

Τούτου χάριν – The phrase is unusual, beginning with χάρις in the accusative case, which functions as a preposition with the genitive case! In contrast to most prepositional phrases, the preposition comes *after* the word it governs. It is technically called an **improper preposition**. Essentially, it means *the word can have multiple functions*.[21] To add further complexity, the accusative singular spelling χάριν for the third declension noun χάρις is unusual: Should it not be χάριτα? Indeed, we find the longer spelling twice in the NT (Acts 24:27; Jude 4), but χάριν in the other forty-two occurrences. It is probably not accidental that God's χάρις is the focus on the unit: perhaps the apostle intends a pun.

ἐγὼ Παῦλος (v. 1) occurs six times in Paul's letters (Gal 5:2; 1 Thess 2:18; 2 Cor 10:1; Eph 3:1; Col 1:23; Phlm 9)—once in each Asia Minor letter. The apostle uses the phrase to enter more emphatically into the discourse.

— εἴ γε – The em dash indicates **anacoluthon** (ἀνακόλουθος "not following"), *an unexpected change in grammatical construction.* (See the discussion of digression above.) It may be more specifically defined as *nominativus pendens*—when "a sentence is begun with what appears to be the subject, but before the verb is reached something else is substituted in word or in thought."[22] The English em dash may convey a surprising turn in the sentence.

Verses two through thirteen comprise one sentence in Greek (189 words). The absence of a verb led a scribe who copied Cod.Bezae to add πρεσβεύω, "I serve as an ambassador" (see 6:20); the Byzantine tradition has κεκαύχημαι, "I have boasted" (see 2 Cor 7:14). But the intended verb occurs at v. 14. The shorter, earlier, more difficult reading is preferred (see 2:1 for the same phenomenon).

προέγραψα ἐν ὀλίγῳ – This statement challenges interpreters. Is Paul referring to an earlier letter, like Galatians, or one that is lost? We know that not all of Paul's letters survived or were included in the *corpus Paulinum*.[23] Wallace speaks of an **immediate past/dramatic Aorist**: "The aorist indicative can be used of an event that happened rather recently. Its force can usually be

---

[19] Byz mss read ἐγενόμην.

[20] Byz mss read τὴν δοθεῖσάν.

[21] The following are some of the more popular: ἅμα, ἄχρι, ἐγγύς, ἐπάνω, ἕως, κύκλῳ, μεταξύ, ὄπισθεν, πλησίον, χάριν, and χωρίς.

[22] Bernard Dupriez, *A Dictionary of Literary Devices,* trans. Albert W. Halsall (Toronto: University of Toronto Press, 1991), 35.

[23] There seem to be four letters presupposed in 1–2 Corinthians; see Col 4:16.

brought out with something like *just now*, as in *just now I told you*."[24] Paul seems to presuppose the vision of the preceding units (2:1–22) and may allude to the wording at 1:17 by repeating ἀποκάλυψις.[25] The verb's root stands behind γραφή, which had become a semi-technical expression for "Scripture" (2 Tim 3:16). Perhaps the apostle is emphasizing the inspired authority of his argument. He is probably not referring to private, but the communal reading of a lector (see Rev 1:3).

ἐν ὀλίγῳ is adverbial ("briefly").

σύνεσις means *intelligence*, but more specifically *acuteness* or even *shrewdness* with an exegetical connotation—insight into Scripture (Luke 2:47; Eph 3:4). **Philo** (ca. 20 BC–AD 50) uses σύνεσις twenty-five times. He claims people come into the fullness of their intellectual and reasoning powers between the ages of 35 and 42 (*Opif.* 103). A quality of this virtue is being able to distinguish between "honorable" and "dishonorable" thoughts and actions (*Opif.* 153–54). The virtue is a gift from God's Spirit (*Gig.* 23, 27). Paul claims the Spirit of Christ gives σύνεσις to his disciples (2 Tim 2:7), which is not the cleverness of the age (1 Cor 1:19). Paul uses the substantive five times (1 Cor 1:19; Eph 3:4; Col 1:9; 2:2; 2 Tim 2:7). Otherwise, it is only spoken of (Luke 2:47) or by Jesus in the *Shema* (Mark 12:33). "Discernment," then, is a suitable translation.[26]

μυστηρίῳ τοῦ Χριστοῦ – The article may convey a titular sense: "mystery of the Christ" or Messiah (1:20; 2:13).

τοῖς υἱοῖς τῶν ἀνθρώπων is a Hebraism (*benēy ha'adam*, בְּנֵי הָאָדָם) for "human beings," often with an emphasis on our finitude and mortality (Gen 11:5; Is 52:14). Paul alluded to the Son as the son of man in Psalm 8 and Dan 7 (1:22). It may also be a more specific reference to prophets like Ezekiel.

τοῖς ἁγίοις ἀποστόλοις αὐτοῦ καὶ προφήταις – If we grant the originality of ἀποστόλοις, as the *SBLGNT* does, the single article implies a close, if not overlapping, relationship between the apostles and prophets, as we saw at 2:20. But ἁγίοις seems out of place as an attributive adjective since it has been used most often as a substantive (1:1, 15, 18; 2:19), including the immediate context (3:8).[27] ἀποστόλοις is absent in Cod.Vat. This shorter reading also occurs in an Old Latin ms (b) and Ambrosiaster (366–384), suggesting it is not an accidental omission. For an apostle to refer to himself as "holy" seems odd. Paul refers to a broader group of "holy ones"

---

[24] *Greek Grammar*, 568.

[25] Wallace notes: "The author is here speaking about the revelation that was made known to him by God, that is, the revelation of peace between Jew and Gentile, of one new body. It is probable that the aorist here, then, refers back to 2:11–22 rather than to an unknown epistle" (*Greek Grammar*, 568). Less likely, but possible is the scenario of the apostle writing something earlier with his own hand, so that the Ephesians knew the letter was genuine (see Col 4:18; 2 Thess 3:17).

[26] In contrast, Larkin suggests "'insight is not the faculty, but the content of comprehension" (*Ephesians*, 50).

[27] But see the attributive at 1:4. Also, v. 8 has a variant.

(1:15; see the variant at 3:8). So contra the *SBLGNT*, I prefer the shorter, more difficult reading, "holy ones" which is also more consistent with the diction of the letter. Presumably, a copyist allowed the similar expression at 2:20 to influence the reading. The unguarded "holy ones" in reference to prophets may have raised an ecclesial concern.

εἶναι τὰ ἔθνη συγκληρονόμα καὶ σύσσωμα καὶ συμμέτοχα τῆς ἐπαγγελίας – The **infinitive** εἶναι is **appositional** to μυστήριον, finally relating its content.[28] The gloss "namely" may be used.[29] The accusative (according to context) τὰ ἔθνη functions as the subject.

The repeated prefixed preposition σύν evokes 2:5–6. It is probably not accidental that the emphasis and content here parallels the emphatic Ἄρα οὖν οὐκέτι ἐστὲ ξένοι καὶ πάροικοι ἀλλὰ ἐστὲ συμπολῖται τῶν ἁγίων καὶ οἰκεῖοι τοῦ θεοῦ (2:19). The adjective σύσσωμος ("belonging to the same body") may be another neologism; it only occurs here and later Christian literature.

The sentence ("period") ends with alliteration: οὗ ἐγενήθην <u>δ</u>ιάκονος κατὰ τὴν <u>δ</u>ωρεὰν τῆς χάριτος τοῦ θεοῦ τῆς <u>δ</u>οθείσης μοι κατὰ τὴν ἐνέργειαν τῆς <u>δ</u>υνάμεως αὐτοῦ.

3:8–13—THE WEALTH OF CHRIST

[8] ἐμοὶ τῷ ἐλαχιστοτέρῳ πάντων [ἁγίων][30] ἐδόθη [31] ἡ [32] χάρις αὕτη [33] — τοῖς ἔθνεσιν εὐαγγελίσασθαι [34] τὸ[35] ἀνεξιχνίαστον πλοῦτος [36] τοῦ Χριστοῦ, [9] καὶ[37] φωτίσαι πάντας τίς ἡ οἰκονομία[38] τοῦ μυστηρίου τοῦ ἀποκεκρυμμένου[39] ἀπὸ τῶν αἰώνων ἐν τῷ θεῷ[40] τῷ τὰ πάντα κτίσαντι, [10] ἵνα γνωρισθῇ νῦν ταῖς ἀρχαῖς καὶ ταῖς ἐξουσίαις ἐν τοῖς ἐπουρανίοις διὰ τῆς ἐκκλησίας ἡ πολυποίκιλος σοφία τοῦ θεοῦ,[41] [11] κατὰ πρόθεσιν τῶν αἰώνων ἣν ἐποίησεν ἐν τῷ Χριστῷ Ἰησοῦ τῷ κυρίῳ ἡμῶν, [12] ἐν ᾧ ἔχομεν τὴν παρρησίαν καὶ προσαγωγὴν[42] ἐν

---

[28] Hoehner, *Ephesians*, 445.

[29] Wallace, *Greek Grammar*, 606.

[30] Although present in the *SBLGNT* without brackets, it is placed in brackers for reasons given below.

[31] This is an instance of the so-called "Divine Passive," which is not so much a grammatical category as a very common phenomenon in the NT.

[32] The article probably evokes the earlier reference (v. 7). It also functions to hold the place of αὕτη.

[33] We find the preposition ἐν after αὕτη in Byz mss.

[34] An aorist middle infinitive, conveying purpose. If the infinitive were passive, the sense could be "so that the unsearchable wealth of Christ is proclaimed among all the Gentiles."

[35] Byz mss read τόν.

[36] The spelling is irregular (see BDAG).

[37] The conjunction is continuative or epexegetical (Larkin, *Ephesians*, 54).

[38] κοινωνία—on the very slim textual support for this KJV reading, see Comfort, *New Testament Text*, 586.

[39] Another instance of the divine passive.

[40] The dative is locative or conveys agency (Larkin, *Ephesians*, 55).

[41] The genitive conveys source.

[42] The Byz tradition presents the substantive as arthrous (τὴν προσαγωγήν). If original, the sense may be anaphoric evoking 2:18. NA[28] does not record this variant!

πεποιθήσει διὰ τῆς πίστεως αὐτοῦ. ¹³ διὸ αἰτοῦμαι μὴ ἐγκακεῖν ἐν ταῖς θλίψεσίν⁴³ μου ὑπὲρ ὑμῶν,⁴⁴ ἥτις⁴⁵ ἐστὶν δόξα ὑμῶν.

ἐλαχιστοτέρῳ – Literally the "leaster," this is an example of the **comparative form functioning as a superlative**. Wallace suggests it was coined for the occasion, a **neologism**.[46]

ἁγίων – This is omitted by P⁴⁶ which reads "least of all (people)." The shorter, earlier reading sharpens the parallelism at v. 9 (πάντας) and fits the evangelistic context. I must disagree with the *SBLGNT*.[47]

τὸ ἀνεξιχνίαστον πλοῦτος τοῦ Χριστοῦ – The rare adjective ἀνεξιχνίαστος appears to be derived from the verb ἐξιχνιάζω, "to explore, search out" (L&S). The negative prefix (ἀν) signifies what is "unsearchable" (NRS). This explains the need for "special revelation."[48]

φωτίσαι πάντας – The NA²⁵ omits πάντας, which explains its absence in the NAS. The omission may have entered the textual tradition through Cod.Sinai, but the reading has good textual support (P⁴⁶, Cod.Vat, Cod.Bezae, and other mss) and provides parallelism for "Gentiles."[49]

τῶν αἰώνων – again (see 2:2) may have a temporal or demonic referent (Col 1:26). Verse 11 suggests the former.

πολυποίκιλος – This word is a two-termination adjective (no distinct spelling for the feminine), describing what is *diverse* or *many-sided* in reference here to God's wisdom.

ἐν ᾧ ἔχομεν τὴν παρρησίαν καὶ προσαγωγὴν ἐν πεποιθήσει διὰ τῆς πίστεως αὐτοῦ. – The clause employs a common alliteration with *pi* (see Heb 1:1-4). If the second article is not original (see above), παρρησίαν and προσαγωγὴν form a hendiadys ("confident entrance") with the former emphasizing the affective side of the action.

πίστεως αὐτοῦ – The genitive πίστεως αὐτοῦ may be subjective, objective, or both (the so-called "plenary genitive"). The KJV reads, "In whom we have boldness and access with confidence by the faith of him"; the ESV, "in whom we have boldness and access with confidence through our faith in him." But a simple possessive makes sense in the context: "in whom we have boldness and confident access to God because of Christ's faithfulness" (NET).

---

[43] The dative conveys reference or respect.

[44] The *inclusio* with v. 1 makes ἡμῶν, the reading of P⁴⁶, less probable.

[45] Or ἥ τις.

[46] *Greek Grammar*, 302–3.

[47] Comfort does not discuss the variant in his *New Testament Text and Translation Commentary*.

[48] Paul may also claim what Christ offers can be found nowhere else—gifts from his "wealth" (πλοῦτος) include "redemption" (1:7), an "inheritance" (1:18), and "grace" (2:7). Or perhaps Christ himself cannot be comprehended without the continual revelation of the Holy Spirit. He may also see Christ as an endless frontier of discovery. Or perhaps he is in the frontier, and we are following his path. Hebrews refers to Jesus as the "pioneer" of our salvation (2:10).

[49] See also Comfort, *New Testament Text*, 586.

πεποίθησις is a state of certainty about something to the extent of placing reliance on it. This naturally describes the finished work of Christ. The diction evokes 2:18.

ACTIVITIES & QUESTIONS

1. Find all the divine passives in this unit. Restate them as active voice claims. For example, τὴν οἰκονομίαν τῆς χάριτος τοῦ θεοῦ τῆς δοθείσης μοι may be restated: "God gave me the stewardship of his grace."

2. How should we translate διὰ τῆς πίστεως αὐτοῦ at v. 12? Translate Gal 2:16, 2:20, and 3:22. What are the theological implications if Paul is referring to Jesus's faith, not ours?

Key Terms: merism, Mars, Markus Barth, epexegetical infinitive, dative of sphere, *unio liturgica*, William Law, the Sinner's Prayer, Jesus Prayer, Prayer of the Heart

Vocabulary

βάθος, ους, τό – depth	νοέω – I think
γνῶσις, εως, ἡ – knowledge	ὀνομάζω – I name
γόνυ, ατος, τό – knee	πατριά, ᾶς, ἡ – family
ἐνεργέω – I work	πλάτος, ους, τό – width
ἐξισχύω – I am fully able	πλήρωμα, ατος, τό – fullness
ἔσω – inside	πλοῦτος, ου, ὁ – wealth
θεμελιόω – I establish firmly	ῥιζόω – I am firmly rooted
κάμπτω – I bow, bend	ὑπερβάλλω – I surpass
καταλαμβάνω – I understand	ὑπερεκπερισσοῦ – so much more than
κραταιόω – I become strong	ὕψος, ους, τό – height
μῆκος, ους, τό – length	χάριν – because of (stands after its object)

Cutting at the Joints: The repetition of δόξα (vv. 16, 21) and emphasis on the Father delimit the unit, which resolves the digression beginning at v. 2. Elements of v. 1 are repeated to alert the hearers (readers). The prayer and benediction complete Paul's extended section of worship, forming *inclusio* with 1:15–23. The unit also anticipates the paranesis (ethical instruction) that occupies the second half of the letter. "Glory" (δόξα) is partly the recognition of someone's virtue and labor, which is actualized in worship.

3:14–19—PRAYER

Despite the thematic echoes of the opening benediction, Paul offers more personal intercession: κάμπτω τὰ γόνατά μου πρὸς τὸν πατέρα. Elijah bent his knees and placed his face between them to pray for rain (1 Kgs 18:42 OG). Hanina ben Dosa, a Rabbinic contemporary of Paul, famous for the gift of healing, took the position for intercessory prayer, as well as the later *Chasidim* or "holy ones."[1]

Three petitions are introduced with ἵνα-clauses (3:16–17, 18–19a, 19b). Paul asks for (1) *power*

---

[1] Perle Epstein, *Kabbalah: The Way of the Jewish Mystic* (New York: Barnes and Noble, 1978), 37.

(δύναμις) through God's presence in the Spirit and Son and (2) *knowledge* of (a) the Father's glory (δόξα) and (b) the Son's love (ἀγάπη). We may call this the effect and motivation of worship. The requests address concupiscence and ignorance.

The language is Trinitarian—Father (v. 14), Spirit (v. 16), and Son (v. 17). Reflection moves from the Father, to the Spirit, to the Son, and back to the Father.

3:14–15—PREPARATION FOR PRAYER

[14] Τούτου χάριν[2] κάμπτω τὰ γόνατά μου πρὸς τὸν 'πατέρα, [15] ἐξ οὗ πᾶσα[3] πατριὰ ἐν οὐρανοῖς[4] καὶ ἐπὶ γῆς ὀνομάζεται,

κάμπτω τὰ γόνατά μου πρὸς τὸν πατέρα is pleonasm, the use of more words than are necessary to convey meaning. The language emphasizes humility.

πατριά, a cognate noun, shares the same root with (and may be derived from) πατήρ in the previous verse, signifying a "people linked over a relatively long period of time by line of descent to a common progenitor" or father.[5] The Jews traced their ethnicity to Abraham and their law or charter to Moses. The Romans looked to Romulus and Remus, who were believed to have been fathered by **Mars**, the god of war. But there is one Father of all, the ground of being and source of all creation.

After πατέρα, several mss read τοῦ κυρίου ἡμῶν Ἰησοῦ χριστοῦ. There are no other occurrences of "the Father" standing on its own in Paul's letters.[6] It is therefore easier to explain the wording as a later gloss than its absence in our earliest manuscript (P[46]) and the original hand of Cod.Sinai. Paul is punning on πατριὰ.[7] The shorter, earlier, more difficult reading is preferred.

ἐν οὐρανοῖς καὶ ἐπὶ γῆς is **merism** (μερισμός), *the combination of two contrasting words to refer to an entirety.* "Heavens and earth" refer to "all things" or the universe. There may be an allusion to Genesis 1:1.[8] For οὐρανοῖς, Muddiman suggests a reference to deceased Christians, who continue to worship God.[9] It was also a belief among some Jews that angels were divided into families (*1 En.* 69:4; 71:1; 106:5; *b. Ber.* 17a; *b. San.* 38b, 98b, 99b). Recognizing the rhetorical device, however, invites us not to be too specific.

ὀνομάζεται – In the passive, the transitive verb often means "receives its name." In the LXX (OG),

---

[2] See note at 3:1.

[3] πᾶσα with an anarthrous noun generally signifies "every" (Moule, *Idiom Book,* 93–94). This contributes to the reading of angelic or demonic families in the heavens. But see 2:21.

[4] A few later mss read as a singular. The more difficult reading, a Semitism, is preferable here.

[5] BDAG s.v. πατριά.

[6] John Muddiman, *The Epistle to The Ephesians* (Peabody, MA: Hendrickson, 2004), 165–66.

[7] Larkin, *Ephesians*, 60.

[8] Tremper Longman, "Merism," in *Dictionary of the Old Testament: Wisdom, Poetry & Writings,* ed. Tremper Longman and Peter Enns (Downers Grove, IL: InterVarsity, 2008), 464–66, esp. 464.

[9] *Ephesians*, 165–66. See Heb 12:23; John 14:2.

it may signify "to be known" (Esth 9:4; *1 Macc* 3:9; 14:10; *EpArist* 124). Naming is an exercise of power.

3:16–17—FIRST REQUEST

16 ἵνα δῷ[10] ὑμῖν κατὰ τὸ πλοῦτος τῆς δόξης[11] αὐτοῦ δυνάμει[12] κραταιωθῆναι διὰ τοῦ πνεύματος αὐτοῦ εἰς τὸν ἔσω ἄνθρωπον, **17** κατοικῆσαι τὸν Χριστὸν[13] διὰ τῆς πίστεως ἐν ταῖς καρδίαις ὑμῶν ἐν ἀγάπῃ· ἐρριζωμένοι καὶ τεθεμελιωμένοι,

κραταιωθῆναι – The infinitive is appositional, relating the content of the apostle's prayer of request. δύναμις reinforces the sense with the dative allowing the noun to function adverbially. The verb κραταιόω (always passive in the NT) describes *the strengthening effect of growth*, one of the two core metaphors for sanctification (or spiritual formation) in the Bible.[14] Luke describes the maturation of Jesus and the Baptist this way (2:40). Concerning the latter, he writes: Τὸ δὲ παιδίον ηὔξανεν καὶ ἐκραταιοῦτο πνεύματι (Luke 1:80). The dative πνεύματι is like διὰ τοῦ πνεύματος. In context, the Gentiles have been recreated (born again) and have joined God's people; the focus becomes maturation. Although there is personal discipline (ἄσκησις) in the Christian life, the apostle stresses divine agency—hence the need for prayer.

εἰς τὸν ἔσω ἄνθρωπον – This prepositional phrase has invited two interpretations. On the one hand, the metaphorical expression may refer to the spiritual (non-material) element of a human being—what is left after the σῶμα. Paul may intend καρδία as a parallel expression in the subsequent clause (see also 1:18). This comports with the two other occurrences of the expression in Paul's letters (2 Cor 4:16; Rom 7:22). On the other, **Markus Barth** (1915–1994) identifies the inner man as Jesus Christ.[15] I suggest a both/and: the inner person is who we are in Christ (Gal 2:20). The language anticipates the mystery of union in marriage (5:22–33). It is the part of us that has already been recreated, joined to the resurrected heart of Christ, yet remains joined to our outer selves, the body and brain.

κατοικῆσαι – The infinitive is epexegetical to κραταιωθῆναι.[16] The adjective epexegetical is perhaps an overly technical way of describing something as "additionally explanatory," an expansion. Wallace notes: "The **epexegetical infinitive** clarifies, explains, or qualifies a noun or adjective. This use of the infinitive is usually bound by certain lexical features of the noun or adjective. That is, they normally are words indicating ability, authority, desire, freedom, hope,

---

[10] Byz mss read δώῃ.

[11] Larkin treats the genitive as epexegetical: "riches, that is, his glory" (*Ephesians*, 61).

[12] The dative conveys manner ("with power").

[13] τὸν Χριστόν functions as the accusative subject of the infinitive.

[14] The other is journey.

[15] *Ephesians*, 2 vols. (NY: Doubleday, 1974), 1:370; see Best, *Ephesians*, 340; Muddiman, *Ephesians*, 168.

[16] Larkin, *Ephesians*, 62.

need, obligation, or readiness."[17] The verb κατοικέω, which is related to οἰκία ("house" or "home"), describes *taking up residence somewhere*. It is God's way residing in a temple. Jesus promised to be with his disciples through the Holy Spirit (John 14:23, with the Spirit in the context). We may add "—that is" as a gloss to our translation.

διὰ τῆς πίστεως – The article may be anaphoric, referring back to v. 12. If so, Christ is able to dwell within us because of his faithfulness, which allowed us in the Holy of Holies. Yet perhaps his faith may become our own (1:15).

ἐν ταῖς καρδίαις ὑμῶν – The **dative of sphere** may refer back to τὸν ἔσω ἄνθρωπον, underscoring that God has now taken up residence in people, both individually and communally, not a building. Wallace notes: "The dative substantive indicates the sphere or realm in which the word to which it is related takes place or exists. Normally this word is a verb, but not always."[18] In this case, the rule applies.

ἐν ἀγάπῃ ἐρριζωμένοι καὶ τεθεμελιωμένοι – Larkin suggests this entire phrase is fronted for emphasis and belongs with the ἵνα clause.[19]

ἐρριζωμένοι καὶ τεθεμελιωμένοι – The perfect tenses suggest a state from a previous action or event. The context suggests they are divine passives: God rooted and founded the Gentiles (see 1 Pet 5:10). (The masculine gender implies Paul is referring to the people, not just their καρδία.) But the phrase ἐν ἀγάπῃ probably answers how God did this—the efficient (or instrumental) cause. Sanctification is overdetermined. The expression may be a hendiadys, with both verbs (ῥιζόω and θεμελιόω) describing the edification of God's people on the foundation of the apostles, prophets, and Jesus Christ (2:20). But ῥιζόω may cut deeper into the bedrock of God. The verb is derived from ῥίζα ("root"). The metaphor suggests the very love of God sustains and grows us (see Rom 5:5). God grows us by sharing his love. This explains the Trinitarian movement of the prayer.

3:18–19A—SECOND REQUEST

[18]ἵνα ἐξισχύσητε[20] καταλαβέσθαι[21] σὺν πᾶσιν τοῖς ἁγίοις τί τὸ πλάτος καὶ μῆκος καὶ ὕψος καὶ βάθος,[22] [19a]γνῶναί τε[23] τὴν ὑπερβάλλουσαν τῆς γνώσεως[24] ἀγάπην τοῦ Χριστοῦ,[25]

---

[17] *Greek Grammar*, 607, emphasis added.

[18] *Greek Grammar*, 153.

[19] *Ephesians*, 62–63.

[20] The emphatic "fully" is derived from the rare occurrence of the prefixed verb ἐξισχύσητε.

[21] The middle voice conveys the subject's necessary role in mental processing.

[22] Cod.Sinai and Byz mss read βάθος καὶ ὕψος. The single article creates an impersonal construction, with "distinct entities, though united" (Wallace, *Greek Grammar*, 286).

[23] This is a rare instance of the τε *solitarium*—there is no finishing καί.

[24] The genitive conveys comparison.

[25] ἀγάπην τοῦ Χριστοῦ is probably a Subjective Genitive—"love which comes from Christ." This love binds

ἵνα ἐξισχύσητε καταλαβέσθαι – ἐξισχύω (ἰσχύω), a NT *hapax legomenon*, describes *the state of being fully capable of doing or experiencing something.*[26] Such verbs often require an infinitive to complete (complement) their sense: καταλαμβάνω (λαμβάνω) *refers to the act of making something one's own.* The translations "comprehend" (KJV) and "grasp" (NIV) capture both sides of the meaning. The infinitive καταλαβέσθαι is in the middle voice, which emphasizes the subject's role in the action.

σὺν πᾶσιν τοῖς ἁγίοις – The phrase conveys association, perhaps with the Jewish wing of the church and/or other Gentile communities but also angels—those who behold God in heaven (see the discussion of ἐν οὐρανοῖς above). We find a **unio liturgica** motif in Jewish apocalyptic literature—worshipful communion with angels in heaven.[27] Christians considered angels as part of their corporate worship. In any case, the substantive adjective refers to the necessary quality possessed by things and persons that could approach divinity—or, in this case, the reverse (see 1:1).

τὸ πλάτος καὶ μῆκος καὶ ὕψος καὶ βάθος – Since the four measurements share the single artiele τό, one referent is probably intended. But it is left unstated. πλάτος refers to *breadth* or width; μῆκος, *length*; ὕψος, *height*; βάθος, *depth*. The final two measurements presuppose a viewpoint from the middle—unable to see the full height or depth of something. The Fathers (Irenaeus, *Haer.* 5.17.4; Augustine, *Doct. Christ.* 2.4.1) see the cross, the symbol of divine love: the saving work of Christ reaches up to heaven, down to hell, and covers the world from east to west (see 2:16; Rom 8:38). The immediate context suggests τὸ πλήρωμα τοῦ θεοῦ. (The Gnostic misappropriation of πλήρωμα may have dissuaded the fathers from this commonsense reading.) We often fail in worship because our God is too small. Paul may appropriate the Greco-Roman assumption that *like sees like* (see 1 John 3:2). Those who are holy may begin to see the Holy God (Matt 5:8). We do not see the Father or the Spirit, but Christ is the image of the invisible God, and he has his hands in everything (Col 1:15–20). God is farther than the stars, but closer than our hearts.

3:19B—THIRD REQUEST

19b ἵνα πληρωθῆτε εἰς[28] πᾶν τὸ πλήρωμα τοῦ θεοῦ.

πληρωθῆτε (from πληρόω) – God is the understood agency ("divine passive"). Notice the redundancy for rhetorical impact with πλήρωμα.

---

and directs the church (Rom 8:35; 2 Cor 5:14).

[26] BDAG s.v. ἰσχύω.

[27] Jody A. Barnard, *The Mysticism of Hebrews: Exploring the Role of Jewish Apocalyptic Mysticism in the Epistle to the Hebrews*, WUNT 2/331 (Tübingen: Mohr Siebeck, 2012), 25–28.

[28] Instead of having πληρωθῆτε εἰς, P⁴⁶, Cod.Vat, and other mss read simply πληρωθῇ omitting the εἰς.

3:20–21—BENEDICTION

This subunit, a short benediction or doxology, completes the first section of the letter. It echoes the earlier prayer (1:15–19).[29] The transition is marked by δέ.

> [20] Τῷ δὲ δυναμένῳ ὑπὲρ[30] πάντα ποιῆσαι ὑπερεκπερισσοῦ[31] ὧν αἰτούμεθα ἢ νοοῦμεν κατὰ τὴν δύναμιν τὴν ἐνεργουμένην ἐν ἡμῖν, [21] αὐτῷ ἡ δόξα ἐν τῇ ἐκκλησίᾳ καὶ ἐν Χριστῷ Ἰησοῦ εἰς πάσας τὰς γενεὰς τοῦ αἰῶνος τῶν αἰώνων· ἀμήν.

ἐν τῇ ἐκκλησίᾳ καὶ ἐν Χριστῷ Ἰησοῦ – The absence of καί in most Byzantine witnesses makes for an interesting variant: "to him be the glory in the church in Christ Jesus." Although consistent with Paul's vision, the language is perhaps too unusual. The older, in this case fuller, reading is preferred.

ἀμήν, somewhat surprisingly the only occurrence in Ephesians, offers a more definitive ending to the prayer. The Greek is an indeclinable transliteration of אָמֵן, which is often translated γένοιτο "may it be."

ACTIVITIES & QUESTIONS

William Law (1686–1761), who impressed George Whitefield and the Wesley brothers, writes:

> Poor Sinner! consider the Treasure thou hast within Thee, the Saviour of the World, the eternal Word of God lies hid in Thee, as a Spark of the Divine Nature, which is to overcome Sin and Death, and Hell within Thee, and generate the Life of Heaven again in thy Soul. Turn to thy Heart, and thy Heart will find its Saviour, its God within itself. Thou seest, hearest, and feelest nothing of God, because thou seekest for Him *abroad* with thy outward Eyes, thou seekest for Him in Books, in Controversies, in the Church, and outward Exercises, but *there* thou wilt not find him, till thou hast *first* found Him in thy Heart. Seek for Him in thy Heart, and thou wilt never seek in vain, for there He dwelleth, there is the Seat of his Light and Holy Spirit.[32]

I came to faith by "inviting Jesus into my heart." **Billy Graham** (b. 1918) popularized this "sinner's prayer":

> *O God, I know that I am a sinner and need Your forgiveness. I believe that You died for my sins. I want to turn from my sins. I now invite You to come into my heart and life. I want to*

---

[29] Larkin, *Ephesians*, 59.

[30] Absent in P[46] and Cod.Bezae.

[31] Byz mss read ὑπὲρ ἐκπερισσοῦ. The preposition with the genitive signifies "so much more than." It can be treated as one word, an adverb ("quite beyond all measure").

[32] *The Spirit of Prayer* 1.2. See Mark A. Noll, *The Rise of Evangelicalism: The Age of Edwards, Whitefield and the Wesleys* (Downers Grove, IL: InterVarsity Press, 2003) 73.

trust You as Savior and follow You as Lord, in the fellowship of Your church. In Christ's name, Amen.[33]

Eventually, I began to ask *how* to seek Jesus in this way. The Orthodox tradition offers **the Jesus Prayer** (Ἡ Προσευχή του Ἰησοῦ): "Lord Jesus Christ, son of God, have mercy on me, the sinner!"[34] The one praying is encouraged to focus inwardly, even lowering one's head to the chest. By grace, over time, the discipline leads to **the prayer of the heart** (Καρδιακή Προσευχή), *the unceasing awareness of and adoration for God's presence.* The anonymous author of *The Way of a Pilgrim* writes:

> The continuous interior prayer of Jesus is a constant uninterrupted calling upon the divine name of Jesus with the lips, in the spirit, in the heart, while forming a mental picture of His constant presence, and imploring His grace, during every occupation, at all times, in all places, even during sleep.[35]

Question: In your opinion, could Eph 3:14–21 serve as a basis for following these practices of prayer? Give specific reasons for or against from these verses.

---

[33] "Death and the Life After," in *The Enduring Classics of Billy Graham* (Nashville, TN: Thomas Nelson, 2002), n.p., emphasis his.

[34] Κύριε Ἰησοῦ Χριστέ, Υἱὲ τοῦ Θεοῦ, ἐλέησόν με τὸν ἁμαρτωλόν.

[35] Trans. R. M. French (New York: Quality Paperback Book Club, 1998), 9.

WEEK 8—EPH 4:1–16

Key Terms: paranesis (is to ought), pleonasm, John Chrysostom, citation formula, *targum*, cognate accusative

Vocabulary

αἰχμαλωσία, ας, ἡ – group of captives	κλῆσις, εως, ἡ – calling
αἰχμαλωτεύω – I capture	κλυδωνίζομαι – I am tossed by the sea
ἀληθεύω – I speak truth	κυβεία, ας, ἡ – craftiness
ἀναβαίνω – I ascend	μακροθυμία, ας, ἡ – patience
ἀνέχομαι – I put up with	μεθοδεία, ας, ἡ – scheme
ἀξίως – worthily	μέτρον, ου, τό – measure
αὐξάνω – I grow	μέχρι – until
αὔξησις, εως, ἡ – growth	μηκέτι – no longer
ἀφή, ῆς, ἡ – ligament	νήπιος, ία, ιον – infant
βάπτισμα, ατος, τό – baptism	οἰκοδομή, ῆς, ἡ – edification
δέσμιος, ου, ὁ – prisoner	πανουργία, ας, ἡ – trickery
διδασκαλία, ας, ἡ – teaching	περιφέρω – I blow about
δόμα, δόματος, τό – gift	πλάνη, ης, ἡ – error, deceit
δωρεά, ᾶς, ἡ – give	πλήρωμα, ατος, τό – fullness
ἐνέργεια, ας, ἡ – working	ποιμήν, ένος, ὁ – shepherd, pastor
ἑνότης, ητος, ἡ – unity	πραΰτης, ητος, ἡ – gentleness
ἐπίγνωσις, εως, ἡ – knowledge	σπουδάζω – I do one's best
ἐπιχορηγία, ας, ἡ – assistance, support	συμβιβάζω – I hold together
εὐαγγελιστής, οῦ, ὁ – evangelist	συναρμολογέω – I join together
ἡλικία, ας, ἡ – maturity	σύνδεσμος, ου, ὁ – bond
καταντάω – I attain	ταπεινοφροσύνη, ης, ἡ – humility
καταρτισμός, οῦ, ὁ – equipping	ὑπεράνω – far above
κατώτερος, α, ον – lower	ὕψος, ους, τό – height

4:1–6:20—PARANESIS

The first major section is dominated by a series of prayers interrupted twice with digressions (1:20–2:22 and 3:2–13). The remaining part of the letter consists of **paranesis** (παραίνεσις), advice and exhortation, the third formal element of the letter.[1] It is a course of action that shapes character. Paul moves from **is to ought**. What does union with Christ look like—in our thoughts, actions, and relationships?[2]

4:1–16—DIVERSE ONENESS IN CHRIST

Cutting at the Joints: The postpositive particle οὖν functions inferentially, evoking the letter's first half. The unit consists of three parts: Paul emphasizes 1) oneness in 4:1–6, 2) diversity in 4:7–10, and 3) oneness again in 4:11–16.[3] The whole appears to celebrate *unity* and *diversity*. The dynamism flows from a Trinitarian approach to God. The unit is paradoxical: oneness is the dominant motif yet there is one Spirit (v. 4), one Lord Jesus Christ (v. 5), and one God and Father (v. 6). The triune God is formally introduced to the world in the one baptism of Jesus Christ.

4:1–6—CALL TO ONENESS

Paul gives the famous list of seven unifying elements of Christianity.[4] The unit mentions all three theological virtues: faith, hope, and love.

4.1 Παρακαλῶ[5] οὖν ὑμᾶς ἐγὼ[6] ὁ δέσμιος ἐν κυρίῳ[7] ἀξίως περιπατῆσαι[8] τῆς κλήσεως ἧς ἐκλήθητε, **2** μετὰ[9] πάσης ταπεινοφροσύνης καὶ πραΰτητος,[10] μετὰ[11] μακροθυμίας,

---

[1] Stanley E. Porter, "A Functional Letter Perspective: Towards a Grammar of Epistolary Form," in *Paul and the Ancient Letter Form*, ed. Stanley E. Porter and Sean A. Adams (Leiden: Brill, 2010), 9–32.

[2] The apostle often moves from "theology" to "ethics," although these are modern terms See, for example, the breaks at Rom 12:1 and 1 Thess 4:1.

[3] Hoehner, *Ephesians*, 521.

[4] Talbert refers to the "seven unifying realities of the faith" (*Ephesians and Colossians*, 108).

[5] The circumflex marks that a contraction has occurred in the contract verb παρακαλέω.

[6] The personal pronoun may be heard as intensive or emphatic—"Therefore, I *myself* exhort you"—although it allows the apposition (ὁ δέσμιος ἐν κυρίῳ).

[7] ἐν κυρίῳ could modify either what precedes—the prisoner in the Lord"—or follows. In the latter, two readings are possible: "to walk in the Lord worthily" or "to walk worthily of the calling that you were called in the Lord" (see 1:11!). I follow virtually all the modern English translations (see NIV, NRSV, ESV). The near parallel at 3:1 seems to require this. It is also the simplest reading and makes sense in the context. In either case, ἐν presumably conveys "sphere"—Paul's union with Christ (Hoehner, *Ephesians*, 504). Yet ESV opts for a Dative of Advantage: "a prisoner for the Lord."

[8] Idiomatic (biblical) expression for "live" (Ps 1:1); the aorist tense invites a comprehensive view of life.

[9] The genitive conveys manner.

[10] Byz mss read πραότητος.

[11] The genitive conveys manner.

ἀνεχόμενοι[12] ἀλλήλων ἐν ἀγάπη,[13] [3]σπουδάζοντες[14] τηρεῖν τὴν ἑνότητα τοῦ πνεύματος[15] ἐν τῷ συνδέσμῳ τῆς εἰρήνης·

Παρακαλῶ – In the context of public worship, this verb means "exhort" or "preach." In the synagogue, after a reading from the Law and Prophets, a qualified teacher (διδάσκαλος) expounded the texts. To Timothy Paul writes: ἕως ἔρχομαι πρόσεχε τῇ ἀναγνώσει, τῇ παρακλήσει, τῇ διδασκαλίᾳ, "Until I come, give attention to the reading [of Scripture], to preaching, to teaching" (1 Tim 4:13). The author of Hebrews describes his project as a "word of exhortation" or "sermon" (τοῦ λόγου τῆς παρακλήσεως, 13:22). We are therefore not surprised when Paul unpacks Psalm 68 in this unit. To understand the meaning of παρακαλέω we may also look to the Greco-Roman world because of the Gentile audience. Charles Talbert notes that the term "was used in antiquity, in the context of the benefactor-benefaction system, to summon, exhort, and encourage those who have received a benefaction (*charis*) to respond appropriately to the giver of the gift."[16]

ἐγὼ ὁ δέσμιος ἐν κυρίῳ repeats the previous transition (3:1). But Paul removes his name and switches from "Christ [Jesus]" to ἐν κυρίῳ to emphasize the authority behind the moral exhortation.[17] κύριος consistently refers to Jesus in the letter (2:21; 4:17; 5:8; 6:1, 10, 21). He is the head of the church, the *pater familias*.

ἀξίως – The adverb qualifies *how* the Ephesians are to walk, echoing contemporary inscriptions that celebrate public works.[18] It is to act befitting one's station—in this case, as part of God's people.

τῆς κλήσεως ἧς ἐκλήθητε / ἐκλήθητε ἐν μιᾷ ἐλπίδι τῆς κλήσεως ὑμῶν – The repetition of the stem is a kind of **pleonasm** (πλεονασμός "more," "too much"), *using more words than are necessary to convey meaning*. Rhetorically, it emphasizes the action, which, in this case, is a divine passive ("God called you!") and adds "dignity and splendor to expression"—*gravitas*.[19] It is common in the Asiatic milieu of Paul's first readers, adopted by later preachers like **John Chrysostom**.

ταπεινοφροσύνη and πραΰτης – These nouns have overlapping meanings around *humility*.[20] The

---

[12] A reciprocal middle. The adverbial participle conveys manner.

[13] ἐν ἀγάπη could modify what precedes or proceeds (see note at 1:4). At issue is the placement of the comma.

[14] In parallel with ἀνεχόμενοι, the participle also conveys manner.

[15] The genitive conveys source.

[16] *Ephesians and Colossians* (Grand Rapids: Baker Academic, 2007), 108.

[17] Muddiman, *Ephesians*, 178.

[18] Except for one occurrence in 3 John (v. 6), only Paul uses the adverb in the NT (Rom 16:2; Phil 1:27; Col 1:10; 1 Thess 2:12).

[19] Thomas Edward Ameringer, *A Study in Greek Rhetoric* (Washington, DC: Catholic University of America Press, 1921), 29.

[20] Paul offers a similar exhortation at 2 Cor 10:1.

former is related to φρόνησις, a way of processing reality. The latter is a fruit of the Spirit (Gal 5:23) as is μακροθυμία (v. 22) and ἀγάπη. In context, the body subordinates itself to its head, the Lord Jesus Christ, who himself embodies this state of mind and modus operandi (Phil 2:1–11).[21]

ἑνότης ("unity") is related to the numeral one (εἷς, μία, ἕν, gen. ἑνός), which is heavily appropriated in the unit. The word signifies "a state of oneness or of being in harmony and accord, unity."[22] Except for a variant in Colossians, ἑνότης reoccurs at v. 13, but nowhere else in the NT.

συνδέσμῳ – The word occurs in both the masculine and neuter forms—σύνδεσμος and σύνδεσμον—and signifies a "fastener" like what holds shops together (*Epistle of Aristeas* 85), or the ligaments of the body (Col 2:19). It echoes δέσμιος (v. 1). The motif of the prefixed preposition emphasizes the communal dimension.

> [4] ἓν σῶμα καὶ ἓν πνεῦμα, καθὼς καὶ[23] ἐκλήθητε ἐν μιᾷ ἐλπίδι τῆς κλήσεως ὑμῶν· [5] εἷς κύριος, μία πίστις, ἓν βάπτισμα· [6] εἷς θεὸς καὶ[24] πατὴρ πάντων, ὁ ἐπὶ πάντων καὶ διὰ πάντων καὶ ἐν ⸀πᾶσιν [ἡμῖν][25].

Ἓν σῶμα refers to the church, the bride of Christ, who is not polygamous—hence the need to bring Jews and Gentiles together.

ἓν πνεῦμα refers to the Holy Spirit (v. 3), but is anarthrous like the body to emphasize quality. The Spirit can be distributed but not separated.

μιᾷ ἐλπίδι refers to the Parousia (return or presence of Christ), of which a down payment has already been given. This helps to balance the realized eschatology in the letter.

εἷς κύριος focuses on Christ, the head of the body.

μία πίστις may refer to the faithfulness of Christ (3:12). Christians do not have many faiths, but aim at the singular path of Christ's faithfulness. However, the sense may also be shared convictions about Christ (Gal 1:23; Rom 1:5).

ἓν βάπτισμα – Christians are also baptized into the death and life of Christ, into the Trinitarian life of God: "in the name of the Father, Son, and Holy Spirit" (Matt 28:19).

πάντων could be a neuter, referring to the "cosmos."[26] But its subordinate position to πατήρ sug-

---

[21] ταπεινοφροσύνη occurs at v. 3 in the Kenosis Hymn.

[22] BDAG s.v. εἷς.

[23] Omitted in Cod.Vat and a few other mss. The reading is significant because the adverbial sense "also" draws attention to the election of the Hebrews and Gentiles. Yet the textual evidence is not strong for the omission (so also Hoehner, *Ephesians*, 515).

[24] A few mss omit. We ran into a similar problem at 1:3. I see no compelling reason to follow the minority reading (so also Hoehner, *Ephesians*, 518).

[25] Although not in the *SBLGNT*, the textual support is fairly strong (Cod.Bezae and Byz). See comment below.

[26] Lincoln, *Ephesians*, 240.

gests a masculine reading—"father of all" people or believers. This is Paul's normal use of Father (Rom 8:15; Gal 4:6; Col 1:2; 2 Thess 2:16; Phlm 3). Many English translations obscure with "all" (e.g., ESV). The apostle earlier affirmed God's paternity concerning all people (3:14–15). Yet if we accept the reading ἡμῖν at v. 6, then Paul focuses specifically on the "church"[27] or "believers."[28]

[ἡμῖν] – The possible reading ἡμῖν is significant because it potentially restricts the God's presence to being in believers—"in all of us." Textual support is fairly strong (Cod.Bezae and Byz). Furthermore, there appears to be a thematic link with the subsequent clause beginning the next subunit—Ἑνὶ δὲ ἑκάστῳ ἡμῶν ἐδόθη. The KJV (NKJV) inexplicably reads "in you all." (Miniscule 1241 reads ἀμήν!)

4:7–10—DIVERSITY

> [7] Ἑνὶ δὲ ἑκάστῳ ἡμῶν ἐδόθη ἡ[29] χάρις κατὰ τὸ μέτρον τῆς δωρεᾶς[30] τοῦ Χριστοῦ.[31] [8] διὸ λέγει· Ἀναβὰς εἰς ὕψος ᾐχμαλώτευσεν αἰχμαλωσίαν,[32] ἔδωκεν δόματα[33] τοῖς ἀνθρώποις. [9] τὸ δὲ Ἀνέβη τί ἐστιν εἰ μὴ ὅτι καὶ κατέβη [πρῶτον][34] εἰς τὰ κατώτερα μέρη[35] τῆς γῆς; [10] ὁ καταβὰς αὐτός ἐστιν καὶ ὁ ἀναβὰς ὑπεράνω πάντων τῶν οὐρανῶν, ἵνα πληρώσῃ τὰ πάντα.

δέ is contrastive with the previous subunit. Paul now focuses on diversity.

διὸ λέγει – "It says" or perhaps "He says." Although Paul obliquely cites Psalm 8 earlier (1:22), this is the first **citation formula**. It spotlights the wording or source—the former being the case here. This formula occurs once more (5:14), but nowhere else in the Pauline corpus.[36] Paul cites Psalm 68, but the Hebrew (MT) and Greek (OG 67:19) traditions read "received gifts." Paul may (1) intentionally alter the text[37] or, more likely, (2) follow an alternative textual tradition.[38]

---

[27] Schnackenburg, *Ephesians*, 167.

[28] Hoehner, *Ephesians*, 519.

[29] The article is present (P[46], MT) and absent in the Alexandrian and Byzantine traditions (Cod.Vat and the original hand of Cod.Bezae). Its omission, perhaps a scribal oversight of the twice-occurring letter (ἐδόθη ἡ), is easier to explain than its addition. If the article is original, it suggests a particular aspect of the noun is being stressed—a "particular enablement given to each believer" (Hoehner, *Ephesians*, 522).

[30] A Subjective Genitive: τὸ μέτρον is implicitly verbal—"according to the gift from Christ, which is measured out…" (Hoehner, *Ephesians*, 523). In Romans Paul claims that "we have gifts that differ according to the grace given to us" (12:6).

[31] The genitive conveys source or agency.

[32] Cod.Vat and Byz mss read καὶ after αἰχμαλωσίαν. Comfort rejects the variant (*Commentary*, 589).

[33] The preposition ἐν occurs after δόματα in some later mss, probably added to clarify the syntax of the dative.

[34] πρῶτον is not included in the *SBLGNT*, but is in Cod.Vat and Byz mss. I believe it should be included.

[35] Omitted in P[46], the original hand of Cod.Bezae, and Byz mss.

[36] The only other occurrence in the NT is Jas 4:6 (citing Prov 3:34).

[37] An option noted by Talbert, *Ephesians and Colossians*, 110.

[38] Rabbis occasionally tweak words to draw out the deeper significance (*sod*) of a passage, but it does not seem

The *targum*, an Aramaic translation of the Hebrew used for reading and preaching in the synagogue, reads, "You, Moses the prophet, ascended to the heavens; you took captivity captive, you learned the words of Torah, you gave them as gifts to the sons of men."[39] The *targum* probably does not go back to the first-century, but the reading may be follow an older tradition. The verbs "to give" or "pass along" and "to receive" were seen as two sides of the same coin (see *m. Abot* 1:1; 1 Cor 15:3).

ἠχμαλώτευσεν αἰχμαλωσίαν – The shared stem (αἰχμαλωτεύω, αἰχμαλωσία) creates a **cognate accusative**. In other words, a verb's object is etymologically related to it. The practice is not valued in English, but in other languages, like Arabic, it is considered good style, conveying emphasis.

αἰχμαλωσία – This noun may be translated abstractly "captivity," but also may refer to "a captured military force," which fits the context (see Josephus, *Ant.* 11.1; Num 31:12; Judg 2:9; *1 Macc.* 9.70; *2 Macc.* 8.10). The **captives** are presumably demonic powers (1:21; 2:2; 6:12). The accusative may also function adverbially, intensifying the force of the action.

τὰ κατώτερα μέρη τῆς γῆς – Some read τῆς γῆς as an epexegetical genitive—"that is, the earth" or genitive of apposition (ESV "the earth"). If μέρη is original (see footnote), the syntax is more difficult.

τὸ . . . ἀνέβη . . . ὁ καταβὰς – It is unusual to modify a conjugated verb with an article. This is usually done with a participle or infinitive. However, Paul wants to "substantivize" the actions as lemmas for commentary. We find the form in biblical commentaries among the Dead Sea Scrolls (*Pesharim*).

4:11–16—ONENESS AGAIN

[11] καὶ αὐτὸς ἔδωκεν[40] τοὺς[41] μὲν[42] ἀποστόλους, τοὺς δὲ προφήτας,[43] τοὺς δὲ εὐαγγελιστάς, τοὺς δὲ ποιμένας καὶ διδασκάλους, [12] πρὸς τὸν καταρτισμὸν τῶν ἁγίων εἰς ἔργον διακονίας, εἰς οἰκοδομὴν τοῦ σώματος τοῦ Χριστοῦ, [13] μέχρι καταντήσωμεν[44] οἱ πάντες εἰς τὴν

to be a common practice. Paul also expects his readers to recognized the passage an authority independent of himself.

[39] The same reading occurs in the *midrash* (*Tehar.* 68.11; Hoehner, *Ephesians,* 526; Talbert, *Ephesians and Colossians,* 110).

[40] P[46] reads δέδωκεν.

[41] Hoehner suggests the article takes on the sense of a demonstrative pronoun, and can be translated "some" (*Ephesians,* 538).

[42] Postpositive conjunction, often untranslated. It generally creates a "one the one hand" and "on the other hand" contrast.

[43] A Predicate Accusative, which presumes a copulative verb "to be." This is the same for εὐαγγελιστάς, ποιμένας, and possibly διδασκάλους.

[44] The subjunctive often occurs after a temporal adverb, conjunction, or preposition (Wallace, *Greek Grammar,* 479–80).

ἑνότητα τῆς πίστεως καὶ τῆς ἐπιγνώσεως τοῦ υἱοῦ⁴⁵ τοῦ θεοῦ, εἰς ἄνδρα τέλειον, εἰς μέτρον ἡλικίας⁴⁶ τοῦ πληρώματος τοῦ Χριστοῦ, ¹⁴ ἵνα μηκέτι ὦμεν νήπιοι, κλυδωνιζόμενοι καὶ περιφερόμενοι παντὶ ἀνέμῳ τῆς διδασκαλίας ἐν τῇ κυβείᾳ τῶν ἀνθρώπων ἐν πανουργίᾳ πρὸς τὴν μεθοδείαν τῆς πλάνης,⁴⁷ ¹⁵ ἀληθεύοντες δὲ⁴⁸ ἐν ἀγάπῃ⁴⁹ αὐξήσωμεν⁵⁰ εἰς αὐτὸν τὰ πάντα,⁵¹ ὅς ἐστιν ἡ κεφαλή, Χριστός,⁵² ¹⁶ ἐξ οὗ πᾶν τὸ σῶμα συναρμολογούμενον καὶ συμβιβαζόμενον διὰ πάσης ἁφῆς τῆς ἐπιχορηγίας κατ᾽ ἐνέργειαν ἐν μέτρῳ ἑνὸς ἑκάστου μέρους τὴν αὔξησιν τοῦ σώματος ποιεῖται εἰς οἰκοδομὴν ἑαυτοῦ ἐν ἀγάπῃ.

αὐτός – This unnecessary subject pronoun emphasizes Jesus's role as giver.

ποιμένας καὶ διδασκάλους – The anarthrous διδασκάλους suggests that a single office (or role) is being described. But this is not an instance of the Granville Sharpe rule because the substantive is a plural. We encountered the same ambiguity at 3:5. This allows at least three interpretations. First, Hoehner suggests the καὶ is explicative (what we have been calling epexegetical)— "that is, teachers."⁵³ In this case, a pastor, by definition, is a teacher. Although there are many references to teachers in the NT, this is the only explicit mention of "pastors" (see Ezek 34:2). It would therefore be natural for Paul to clarify his sense. Second, Wallace suggests the first is a subset of the second—all pastors must teach, but not all teachers are pastors.⁵⁴ Third, the omission may simply be intended to avoid redundancy.⁵⁵ I believe the first interpretation is the most plausible. Where would a non-teaching pastor fit in Paul's ecclesiology? Mark's Gospel sees a close relationship between shepherding and teaching:

Mark 6:34 Καὶ ἐξελθὼν εἶδεν πολὺν ὄχλον καὶ ἐσπλαγχνίσθη ἐπ᾽ αὐτούς, ὅτι ἦσαν ὡς πρόβατα μὴ ἔχοντα <u>ποιμένα</u>, καὶ ἤρξατο <u>διδάσκειν</u> αὐτοὺς πολλά.

Paul emphasizes teaching in the unit: παντὶ ἀνέμῳ τῆς διδασκαλίας (v. 14), ἀληθεύοντες, a circumlocution for teaching (v. 15), συμβιβαζόμενον can signify holding together and teaching (v. 16).

πρὸς τὸν καταρτισμὸν τῶν ἁγίων – Within the unit's context, this prepositional phrase may echo

---

⁴⁵ The genitive phrase τοῦ υἱοῦ is omitted in some later mss.

⁴⁶ A Subjective Genitive ("the measured out maturity").

⁴⁷ We find τοῦ διαβόλου after πλάνης in Cod.Alex. The variant is probably a transference from 6:11.

⁴⁸ Instead of ἀληθεύοντες δέ... , two later codices read ἀλήθειαν δὲ ποιοῦντες.

⁴⁹ The dative conveys manner (Larkin, *Ephesians*, 82).

⁵⁰ This is an instance of a hortatory subjunctive "Let us do this or that…" which is equivalent to a first person imperative form that Koine Greek does not have.

⁵¹ The accusative conveys respect (Wallace, *Greek Grammar*, 203). It restricts the reference of the action.

⁵² The second hand of Cod.Sin, Cod.Bezae, Byz, and a few other witnesses read ὁ Χριστός. The arthrous occurrence of the title at v. 13 probably influenced the variant.

⁵³ *Ephesians*, 543.

⁵⁴ *Greek Grammar*, 284.

⁵⁵ Muddiman, *Ephesians*, 199.

Jesus: "A disciple is not above (his or her) teacher.[56] But everyone, after being trained [healed] (καταρτίζω), will be like his (or her) teacher" (Luke 6:40). The verb καταρτίζω may describe restoring something to its proper function and strength training.[57]

ἡλικίας (from ἡλικία, -ας, ἡ) – This noun refers to physical, mental, and spiritual maturity and contrasts with νήπιοι at v. 14.

τῆς διδασκαλίας – This genitive noun contrasts with the Lord's gift of true teachers (v. 11).

SPECIAL NOTE ON 4:16

Verse 16 may be the most difficult to translate in the book:

16 ἐξ οὗ πᾶν τὸ σῶμα συναρμολογούμενον καὶ[58] συμβιβαζόμενον[59] διὰ πάσης ἀφῆς τῆς ἐπιχορηγίας κατ᾽ ἐνέργειαν ἐν μέτρῳ ἑνὸς ἑκάστου μέρους τὴν αὔξησιν τοῦ σώματος ποιεῖται[60] εἰς οἰκοδομὴν ἑαυτοῦ ἐν ἀγάπῃ.

Suggested translation: "from whom the whole body, which is joined and held together by means of every supporting joint, according to the working by means of each individual part, causes the growth of the body for its building up by means of love."

ἐξ οὗ – The relative pronoun phrase ἐξ οὗ links its clause to the preceding with the antecedent being Χριστός (v. 15).

τὸ σῶμα – The subject of the clause is τὸ σῶμα. It is initially modified by πᾶν, which generally does not occur in the attributive position, but clearly has that sense: "from whom the whole body."

συναρμολογούμενον καὶ συμβιβαζόμενον – The subject (τὸ σῶμα) is followed by two adjectival participles functioning attributively: "from whom the whole body, *which is joined and held together*." Note the congruency features in the suffixes. The sense may be conveyed by relative clauses in English translation.

διὰ πάσης ἀφῆς ... κατ᾽ ἐνέργειαν ἐν μέτρῳ – Here we encounter ambiguities with these three prepositional phrases that may modify the preceding participles or the subsequent finite verb ποιεῖται. But the intervening accusative τὴν αὔξησιν suggests the former.

διὰ πάσης ἀφῆς τῆς ἐπιχορηγίας – The first prepositional phrase conveys *secondary agency*, an-

---

[56] The pronoun "his" is absent in our earlier manuscripts. Yet the article identifies a specific teacher.

[57] Literally, Jesus calls James and John while they are "restoring" or "mending" their nets (Mark 1:19; Matt 4:21). But people too need mending (Gal 6:1). The Stoic teacher Epictetus uses καταρτίζω for athletic conditioning (*Diatr.* 3.20.10).

[58] The conjunction may be taken as epexegetical.

[59] The *nu* (ν) switches to a *mu* (μ) with this verb (Larkin, *Ephesians*, 83).

[60] A middle voice, causative construction: "cause growth" (Wallace, *Greek Grammar*, 412). Since the subject acts on itself, this is probably a direct middle.

swering the question "How?" The genitive τῆς ἐπιχορηγίας may be an attributive or epexegetical.[61] The former is simpler. So we now have: "from whom the whole body, which is joined and
held together *by means of every supporting joint*."

κατ᾽ ἐνέργειαν – The second prepositional phrase conveys the manner or standard in which The
brevity of the phrase may explain the variant at P[46]. Of course, the papyrus may preserve the
original.

ἐν μέτρῳ ἑνὸς ἑκάστου μέρους – The third prepositional phrase conveys secondary (instrumental)
agency, like the first phrase—typical Asiatic redundancy. So we now have: "from whom the
whole body, which is joined and held together *by means of every supporting joint, according to
the working by means of each individual part*."

The predicate is τὴν αὔξησιν τοῦ σώματος ποιεῖται εἰς οἰκοδομὴν ἑαυτοῦ ἐν ἀγάπη.

τὴν αὔξησιν τοῦ σώματος conveys the direct object of the transitive verb ποιεῖται. The genitive
is attributive.

ποιεῖται – This verb may be in the passive or middle voice. The reflexive pronoun and context
suggest the latter, which is probably a causative construction: "cause growth."[62] Since the subject acts on itself, this is probably a Direct Middle.

εἰς οἰκοδομὴν ἑαυτοῦ – The prepositional phrase functions adverbially, conveying the purpose or
goal of the action and thus answering the question "Why?"

ἐν ἀγάπη – This prepositional phrase may form an *inclusio* with v. 2. The phrase may modify the
verbal noun οἰκοδομὴν or the main verb ποιεῖται, conveying an instrumental sense.

ACTIVITIES & QUESTIONS

1. Translate Matthew 11:28–30 (provided below). What do these two units have in common?

[28] Δεῦτε πρός με πάντες οἱ κοπιῶντες καὶ πεφορτισμένοι, κἀγὼ ἀναπαύσω ὑμᾶς. [29]
ἄρατε τὸν ζυγόν μου ἐφ ὑμᾶς καὶ μάθετε ἀπ ἐμοῦ, ὅτι πραΰς εἰμι καὶ ταπεινὸς τῇ
καρδίᾳ, καὶ εὑρήσετε ἀνάπαυσιν ταῖς ψυχαῖς ὑμῶν· [30] ὁ γὰρ ζυγός μου χρηστὸς καὶ τὸ
φορτίον μου ἐλαφρόν ἐστιν (Matt 11:28–30, *SBLGNT*).

---

[61] Larkin, *Ephesians*, 83.
[62] Wallace, *Greek Grammar*, 412.

2. John Chrysostom claims Jesus descended into Hades to take Satan, death, sin, and the curse captive. This is his exegesis of 4:9–10:

> When thou hearest these words, think not of a mere removal from one place to another; for what Paul establishes in the Epistle to the Philippians (Phil. ii: 5-8, that very argument is he also insisting upon here. In the same way as there, when exhorting them concerning lowliness, he brings forward Christ as an example, so does he here also, saying, "He descended into the lower parts of the earth." For were not this so, this expression which he uses, "He became obedient even unto death" (Phil. ii.: 8, 9, were superfluous; whereas from His ascending, he implies His descent, and by "the lower parts of the earth," he means "death," according to the notions of men; as Jacob also said, "Then shall you bring down my gray hairs with sorrow to the grave." (Gen. xxxii. 48). And again as it is in the Psalm, "Lest I become like them that go down into the pit" (Ps. cxliii. 7), that is like the dead. Why does he descant upon this region here? And of what captivity does he speak? Of that of the devil; for He took the tyrant captive, the devil, I mean, and death, and the curse, and sin. Behold His spoils and His trophies.
>
> "Now this, He ascended, what is it but that He also descended?"
>
> This strikes at Paul of Samosata and his school.
>
> "He that descended, is the same also that ascended far above all the Heavens, that He might fill all things."
>
> He descended, sayith he, into the lower parts of the earth, beyond which there are none other: and He ascended up far above all things, to that place, beyond which there is none other. This is to show His divine energy, and supreme dominion. For indeed even of old had all things been filled. (*Homilies on Ephesians* 11).[63]

Question: How would evaluate his interpretation on the basis of your own exegesis?

3) What is the relationship between ποιμένας and διδασκάλους? Are they the same role or distinct? What are the implications for the local pastor?

---

[63] Philip Schaff, ed., *Saint Chrysostom: Homilies on Galatians, Ephesians, Philippians, Colossians, Thessalonians, Timothy, Titus, and Philemon,* vol. 13 of *A Select Library of The Nicene and Post-Nicene Fathers of The Christian Church,* trans. Gross Alexander (Grand Rapids: Eerdmans, 1983), 104.

WEEK 9—EPH 4:17–24

Key Terms: resumptive conjunction, epexegetical καί, em dash, final emphasis, fronting, chreia, transitive verb, middle-passive ambiguity

Vocabulary

ἄγνοια, ας, ἡ – ignorance	κτίζω – I create
ἀκαθαρσία, ας, ἡ – impurity	μανθάνω – I learn
ἀνανεόω – I renew	μαρτύρομαι – I testify, witness
ἀναστροφή, ῆς, ἡ – manner of life	ματαιότης, ητος, ἡ – futility
ἀπαλγέω – I become callous, am despondent	μηκέτι – no longer
ἀπαλλοτριόω – I separate	νοῦς, νοός, ὁ – mind
ἀπάτη, ης ἡ – deception	ὁσιότης, τητος, ἡ – holiness
ἀποτίθημι – I put away	παλαιός, ά, όν – old
ἀσέλγεια, ας, ἡ – sensuality	πλεονεξία, ας, ἡ – greed
γέ – indeed	πρότερος, α, ον – former
διάνοια, ας, ἡ – understanding	πώρωσις, εως, ἡ – dullness, obstinacy
ἐνδύω – I put on	σκοτόω – I become dark
ἐργασία, ας, ἡ – practice	φθείρω – I corrupt

Cutting at the Joints: οὖν is a **resumptive conjunction**—pointing back to 4:1–3.[1] The unit repeats a few elements from the exhortation, such as the authority of the Lord Jesus Christ and motifs of walking (living) and redemption of Israel. For Paul, the individual mind and corporate life of the Gentiles are flawed and hostile to God's will. Ignorance and willfulness are the primary agents. The unit follows the "two ways" approach of Jewish ethics. Echoing earlier parts of the letter, the unit may be divided into a before (vv. 17–19) and after (vv. 20–24) sections.

4:17–24—TAKE OFF ADAM; PUT ON CHRIST

This unit describes the profound transformation possible by putting on Christ.

---

[1] Larkin, *Ephesians*, 86. BDAG s.v. offers this entry: "οὖν serves to resume a subject once more after an interruption: *so, as has been said* ἔλεγεν οὖν τοῖς ἐκπορευομένοις Lk 3:7 (connecting w. vs. 3). Cp. 19:12; J 4:6, 9, 28; Ac 8:25; 12:5; cp. 25:4 (s. 4 below).—Cp. 1 Cor 8:4 (reaching back to vs. 1); 11:20."

4:17–19—Then

17 Τοῦτο² οὖν λέγω καὶ μαρτύρομαι ἐν κυρίῳ, μηκέτι ὑμᾶς³ περιπατεῖν καθὼς καὶ 'τὰ ἔθνη περιπατεῖ⁴ ἐν ματαιότητι⁵ τοῦ νοὸς αὐτῶν, **18** ἐσκοτωμένοι⁶ τῇ διανοίᾳ⁷ ὄντες,⁸ ἀπηλλοτριωμένοι τῆς ζωῆς τοῦ θεοῦ,⁹ διὰ τὴν ἄγνοιαν τὴν¹⁰ οὖσαν ἐν αὐτοῖς, διὰ¹¹ τὴν πώρωσιν τῆς καρδίας¹² αὐτῶν, **19** οἵτινες ἀπηλγηκότες¹³ ἑαυτοὺς¹⁴ παρέδωκαν τῇ ἀσελγείᾳ εἰς ἐργασίαν ἀκαθαρσίας πάσης ἐν πλεονεξίᾳ.¹⁵

Τοῦτο οὖν λέγω <u>καὶ</u> μαρτύρομαι – Larkin classifies this as an **epexegetical καί**.¹⁶ Epexegesis is the addition of a word or words to explain a preceding word or sentence. It *generally moves from the abstract to the concrete*, and may be conveyed with an **em dash** and clarifying element: "—that is," or "—namely."¹⁷

καὶ μαρτύρομαι ἐν κυρίῳ – This statement is pleonastic: the formality may evoke a court scene.¹⁸ Paul testifies, although μαρτύρομαι may also mean "to insist."

---

² The pronoun functions as a direct object, but points forward to its clausal postcedent—μηκέτι (Larkin, *Ephesians*, 85).

³ The accusative pronoun functions as the subject of the infinitive (Wallace, *Greek Grammar*, 192–197). The antecedents are believers who were once Gentiles.

⁴ A gnomic present—the description is not of a specific action but a timeless reality.

⁵ The dative conveys manner, answering how they walk (live).

⁶ Cod.Bezae, Byz, and a few mss read ἐσκοτισμένοι (from σκοτίζω). Other witnesses read ἐσκοτωμένοι (from σκοτόω). Both verbs share the same root and occur only in the passive voice in the NT. Paul uses σκοτίζω twice in Rom (1:21; 11:10, a citation from Ps 68:23 OG) in a similar context. This would be the only occurrence of σκοτόω in the *corpus Paulinum*, making it the more difficult reading. In any case, the semantic range of both verbs is essentially the same. A divine passive is probably intended—"God darkened their thinking."

⁷ The dative conveys manner.

⁸ A periphrastic use of the participle (see 2:5, 8).

⁹ The genitive conveys source.

¹⁰ The article functions like a relative pronoun (Wallace, *Greek Grammar*, 213–14).

¹¹ Causal, clarifying the first prepositional phrase.

¹² The genitive is attributed (Wallace, *Greek Grammar*, 91). The head noun functions as the adjective ("hardened heart").

¹³ Elided periphrastic use of the participle. Cod.Bezae and a few other mss read ἀπηλπικότες (ἀπελπίζω), "despair of oneself." Earlier witnesses read ἀπηλγηκότες (ἀπαλγέω).

¹⁴ Fronted for emphasis. The reflexive pronoun was standing in the place of the middle voice. They essentially betrayed and enslaved themselves.

¹⁵ Cod.Bezae and a few other mss read καὶ πλεονεξίας. The more difficult reading is preferred.

¹⁶ *Ephesians*, 86.

¹⁷ John K. Goodrich, *Paul as an Administrator of God in 1 Corinthians* (Cambridge: Cambridge University Press, 2012), 139. The em dash (—) is longer than the en dash (–) and smaller than a hyphen (-). The em dash is perhaps the most versatile punctuation mark, essentially adding a pause to the text.

¹⁸ Today, the work of preachers and lawyers often take place in different buildings, but that was not the case in the synagogue where a local Sanhedrin met. Paul recommends this practice to the Corinthian church over against going to local courts (1 Cor 6). For more discussion, see Bertrand A. Wilberforce, *A Devout Commentary on The Epistle to the Ephesians* (Saint Louis, MO: B. Herder, 1902), 162.

τὰ ἔθνη – In Byz and "corrections" in Cod.Sinai and Cod.Bezae we find the longer reading τὰ λοιπὰ ἔθνη "the other Gentiles/nations." The adjective λοιπά was probably added as a qualification from an ambiguity over the religious and ethnic sense of Gentiles. The earlier, shorter, and more difficult reading is preferred.

ματαιότης ("vanity") may echo the motif in Ecclesiastes (1:2 OG).

ἐσκοτωμένοι ... ἀπηλλοτριωμένοι ... ἀπηλγηκότες – These perfect participles are intensive, highlighting the present state of affairs (review Week 4).

τὴν πώρωσιν τῆς καρδίας αὐτῶν ("their hardness of heart") may evoke the Jesus tradition (Mark 3:5), although the expression is stock apocalyptic language (e.g., *1 Enoch* 5.4), describing being closed off from God in the seat of the soul. Jesus and the Prophets warned against this congenital heart condition, the center of sensory experience. In the Gospels, the hardening is the conscious refusal to believe in Jesus, getting off track in discipleship (see Mark 8:14–21 and parallels) and blaspheming **the Holy Spirit** (Mark 3:29; 4:12).

ἀπηλλοτριωμένοι τῆς ζωῆς – The genitive often conveys separation (review week 5). This is the only occurrence of ζωή ("life") in the letter, although we find the cognate verb συζωοποιέω ("make alive together with") in an earlier, parallel section (2:5). The word often connotes new, full, or spiritual life in the NT, but only in relation to God.

ἀπηλγηκότες – BDAG finds an ambiguity for ἀπαλγέω:

> **1. to be so inured that one is not bothered by the implications of what one is doing, *become callous, dead to feeling,*** without a sense of right and wrong (Polyb. 16, 12, 7; cp. Nägeli 34) ἀπηλγηκότες *dead to all feeling* (REB; so, with variations, most translations) **Eph 4:19.** For a difft. perspective s. 2.

> **2. to be filled with a heavy sense of loss or deprivation, *be despondent*** (Polyb. 1, 35, 5 ἀπηλγηκυίας ψυχάς; Cass. Dio 48, 37) **Eph 4:19** (cp. the v.l. ἀπηλπικότες 'despairing', and cp. 2:12 ἐλπίδα μὴ ἔχοντες; their hopelessness leads them into vice: ἑαυτοὺς παρέδωκαν τῇ ἀσελγείᾳ). S. 1 above.

ἀσελγεία – This term may refer to homosexual behavior, an expression of "lust" (πλεονεξία).[19] It characterizes Sodom and Gomorrah (2 Pet 2:7).

ἐν πλεονεξίᾳ – "in greediness" occurs in a final placement for **final emphasis**, which is the last thing impressed on the audiences' mind. BDAG indicates that this noun means "the state of desiring to have more than one's due, *greediness, insatiableness, avarice, covetousness.*" Translations vary greatly in rendering this prepositional phrase. Greediness was not an acceptable disposition or attribute in the Greco-Roman world.

---

[19] G. Thomas Hobson, "ἀσελγείᾳ in Mark 7:22," *Filologia Neotestamentaria* 21 (2008): 65–74, esp. 67. See Rom 13:13.

4:20–24—NOW

²⁰ ὑμεῖς δὲ οὐχ οὕτως ἐμάθετε τὸν Χριστόν,²⁰ ²¹ εἴ γε²¹ αὐτὸν ἠκούσατε καὶ ἐν αὐτῷ ἐδιδάχθητε,²² καθώς ἐστιν ἀλήθεια²³ ἐν τῷ Ἰησοῦ, ²² ἀποθέσθαι ὑμᾶς κατὰ τὴν προτέραν ἀναστροφὴν τὸν παλαιὸν ἄνθρωπον τὸν φθειρόμενον²⁴ κατὰ τὰς ἐπιθυμίας²⁵ τῆς ἀπάτης, ²³ ἀνανεοῦσθαι δὲ²⁶ τῷ²⁷ πνεύματι τοῦ νοός²⁸ ὑμῶν, ²⁴ καὶ ἐνδύσασθαι τὸν καινὸν ἄνθρωπον τὸν²⁹ κατὰ θεὸν κτισθέντα ἐν δικαιοσύνῃ καὶ ὁσιότητι τῆς ἀληθείας.³⁰

δέ – The δέ marks a transition to the second subunit. The before and after picture is reapplied (2:1–22), but now with the specific exhortation to be renewed by the Spirit of your mind (see Rom 12:1–12).[31] We are being metamorphosed from the inside (inner person) out (resurrected body) into a new way of being human. Someday, we shall have his body, but now enjoy his mind.

ὑμεῖς δὲ οὐχ οὕτως ἐμάθετε τὸν Χριστόν – This is a unique expression, yet a disciple (μαθητής) would learn (μανθάνω) his or her teacher. This resolves the earlier allusion to the Jesus tradition in these nouns describing the virtues Paul expects of believers: μετὰ πάσης ταπεινοφροσύνης καὶ πραΰτητος (4:2; cf. Matt 11:28–30). Humility and gentleness epitomize Christ.

ὑμεῖς is fronted. **Fronting** is any construction where a word group that usually follows the verb is placed at the start of a sentence for emphasis. A subject pronoun's default position is immediately following the verb.[32] In general, the more to the left a word occurs the more emphatic it is.

---

[20] Possibly an Accusative of Respect, but more likely a direct object (see 4:21). The clause is litotes. "Christ" may be metonymy for Christian teaching (Larkin, *Ephesians*, 90).

[21] Byz mss read εἴγε. The two (or one) particle(s) do not signify doubt, but may be translated "because" (Aquinas; cited in Wilberforce, *A Devout Commentary*, 166) or less aggressively, "if, as I take for granted" (Charles Hodge, *A Commentary on The Epistle to The Ephesians* (NY: Robert Corter & Brothers, 1878), 257).

[22] This and the previous aorist verbs ἐμάθετε and ἠκούσατε take a perfective viewpoint on the action, which allows a completed action in the past. Paul may refer to their hearing of the gospel and introductory catechesis before or after baptism.

[23] Some commentators suggest Paul intended a dative (ἀληθείᾳ). This reading is in the margin of the earlier Westcott and Hort text. The sense would be "he [Christ] is in truth [truly] in Jesus." But this presupposes a split between the two, which is foreign to Paul's thought (Hoehner, *Ephesians*, 596). The absence of an article may emphasize quality.

[24] The article functions like a relative pronoun (Wallace, *Greek Grammar*, 213–14).

[25] Cod.Bezae and a few other witnesses read τὴν ἐπιθυμίαν.

[26] P⁴⁹ reads ἐν after δέ.

[27] Some take the dative as reference (Lincoln *Ephesians*, 286). But if a passive is intended, an instrumental makes better sense: "by the spirit of your mind." In this case, *pneuma* probably stands for the human spirit or inner person (Larkin, *Ephesians*, 93).

[28] Larkin treats the genitive as epexegetical—a specific example of which the head noun names a category (*Ephesians*, 93). This is like the Partitive Genitive. In any case, the mind is an element of the inner person.

[29] The article functions like a relative pronoun (Wallace, *Greek Grammar*, 213–14).

[30] The original hand of Cod.Bezae and a few other mss read καὶ ἀλήθεια.

[31] Larkin points out contrasting parallelism (*Ephesians*, 91).

[32] Martin M. Culy, Mikeal C. Pasons, and Joshua J. Stigall, *Luke: A Handbook on the Greek Text* (Waco, TX: Baylor University Press, 2010), xxxii.

Paul orchestrates repetition of reference to Christ with a chiasm:

A ὑμεῖς δὲ οὐχ οὕτως ἐμάθετε τὸν Χριστόν εἴ γε

    B αὐτὸν ἠκούσατε καὶ

    B' ἐν αὐτῷ ἐδιδάχθητε

A' καθώς ἐστιν ἀλήθεια ἐν τῷ Ἰησοῦ

The structure clarifies what it means to learn Christ—to adopt the ultimate reality (truth) he teaches, but also to reflect our union with him. The apostle presupposes catechesis with Jesus as "the only teacher" (Ignatius of Antioch). The language alludes to 1:13 with its celebration of baptism.

τῷ Ἰησοῦ – The article may emphasize the particularity of Jesus's historical ministry.

ἀποθέσθαι (from ἀποτίθημι) – The middle voice is common with verbs of grooming—in this case, "taking off" (metaphorical) clothing. The metaphor is apt because clothing was essential to identifying one's social class and social identity.

There is debate whether the infinitive conveys an imperative or indicative sense. The aorist takes a perfective view of the action, which suggests either a past event or *particular* command. Wallace translates: "you have been taught in him…that you have put off…the old man."[33] In contrast, the MacDonald Idiomatic Translation reads: "Strip off the old self that characterized your former lifestyle, corrupted as it is by deceitful impulses." The former reading clearly has more supporters. But the debate is unnecessary for this reason: Even if Paul appeals to a past reality, there is an implied exhortation—be who you are! (see v. 17). The language is similar to Paul's exhortation to the Romans that has imperative verbs (12:1–2).

Like we saw at 3:7, the infinitive is probably appositional to ἠκούσατε, conveying the content of discipleship: "But you did not learn Christ this way—namely, to put off."

Understanding the broader philosophical background may help clarify the exhortation. The ancient biographer Diogenes Laertius records this episode as a **chreia**, a short pithy story of an important historical figure concluding with a wise action or statement: "When Pyrrho was attacked by a dog, he sought refuge in a tree, which was inconsistent with his philosophy (or truth). When someone pointed out the hypocrisy, he said: 'It is difficult to put off entirely the man [ἄνθρωπον].' (*Lives of the Philosophers* 9.66)[34]

ἀνανεοῦσθαι – The switch to the present from the previous aorist infinitive (ἀποθέσθαι) brings

---

[33] *Greek Grammar*, 605. The NET has a slightly different wording: "You were taught with reference to your former way of life to lay aside the old man who is being corrupted in accordance with deceitful desires."

[34] The Greek for the translation may be found in Diogenes Laertius, *Lives of Eminent Philosophers*, 2 vols., trans. R. D. Hicks (Cambridge, MA: Harvard University Press, 2000), 2:478. Hicks translates ἄνθρωπον as "human weakness."

imperfective aspect to the action, which, as the context suggests, allows for continuous *Aktion-sart*.[35] The break in the parallelism, along with δέ, suggests Paul added this internal, dynamic dimension to our new identity in Christ. It is more than a change of clothing. We have to see a better way and be led by the Spirit.

A **transitive verb**, ἀνανεόω describes *the act of renewing something*; intransitive, *becoming young again*.[36] *A transitive verb requires a direct object* (often in the accusative case, but also the genitive and, occasionally, the dative) *to complete its meaning*. This leads to a **middle-passive ambiguity** because the present (in contrast to the aorist) can be either. Should we read ἀνανεοῦσθαι as a middle/intransitive or a passive/transitive? BDAG suggests the latter:

> The act. is not found very oft. w. this mng. [renew] (in a dedication to Aristonous of Corinth [III BC] fgm. 2b Diehl[2] [AnthLG II, 6 p. 139] Δελφοὶ ἀνενέωσαν τὰν πάτριον προξενίαν; M. Ant. 4, 3, 3 σεαυτόν; 6, 15, 1; Herm. Wr. 9, 6; ins; pap; Job 33:24; 1 Macc 12:1; Iren., 3, 3, 3 [Harv. II 11, 1]) ἀ. τὴν ζωήν (of the angel of repentance) *restore life* Hs 9, 14, 3. Much more freq. (since Thu. 7, 33, 4) is the mid. (Diod. S. 33, 28a, 3 Dind.; 37, 15, 2; Chion, Ep. 16, 8; Appian, Maced. 11 §6; SIG 721, 13; 475, 10; 554, 6; 591, 53, cp. index; OGI 90, 35; Esth 3:13b; 1 Macc 12:3, 10, 16 al.; Jos., Bell. 1, 283, Ant. 1, 290), which seems not to have the reflexive sense 'renew oneself'. Hence ἀνανεοῦσθαι τῷ πνεύματι τοῦ νοός is better taken as a pass. *be renewed=(let yourselves) be renewed in the spirit of your minds* **Eph 4:23** (on the figure Cornutus 33 p. 70, 10 ἀνανεάζειν ἐκ τῶν νόσων καὶ ἐκδύεσθαι τὸ γῆρας). ἀνανεοῦται τὸ πνεῦμα *his spirit is renewed* Hv 3, 12, 2; 3, 13, 2, cp. 3, 12, 3.

ἐνδύσασθαι – Some of our earliest witnesses (P[46], Cod.Sinai, Cod.Vat) read ἐνδύσασθε, an imperative form. We find this same imperative form at Eph 6:11, Rom 13:14, and Col 3:12. Yet ἐνδύσασθαι also occurs in the papyri (P[49]) and has strong attestation in the Western (original hand of Cod.Bezae) and Byzantine traditions.[37] The infinitive is also the more difficult reading. It is easier to imagine the form being switched to an imperative than the reverse. As with ἀποθέσθαι (v. 22), the middle voice is common with verbs of grooming—in this case, "putting on" (metaphorical) clothing. Following baptism, all Christians wore the same white garment.

If τῆς ἀληθείας is original (see footnote), the article is anaphoric, referring back to ἀλήθεια ἐν τῷ Ἰησοῦ (v. 21).

---

[35] Talbert suggests "continually renewed" (*Ephesians and Colossians*, 124; see also Larkin, *Ephesians*, 92).

[36] BDAG s.v. ἀνανεόω.

[37] See Hoehner, *Ephesians*, 609.

ACTIVITIES & QUESTIONS

1. The verb ἀπαλγέω may signify "becoming callous" or "despondent." Which makes better sense in the context? What are the implications for how we serve non-Christians?

2. The prepositional phrase ἐν πλεονεξίᾳ "in greediness" is translated quite differently among the major English translations. Compare three or more translations. What various possible meanings of the phrase are these translations trying to convey? Which meaning(s) do you think are most likely present here in context?

3. What are the soteriological implications of Paul's vacillation between the aorist and present infinitives and the voice of ἀνανεοῦσθαι in vv. 22–24? In other words, how might the change from aorist to present tense and back to aorist shape your understanding of salvation and discipleship?

WEEK 10—EPH 4:25–5:2

Key Terms: present imperative tense, intertextuality, adversative καί, *codices recentiores—non deteriores*

Vocabulary

ἀπολύτρωσις, εως, ἡ – redemption	μηκέτι – no longer
ἀποτίθημι – I put away	μιμητής, οῦ, ὁ – imitator
βλασφημία, ας, ἡ – slander	οἰκοδομή, ῆς, ἡ – edification, encouragement
ἐπιδύω – I set	ὀργίζω – I am angry
εὔσπλαγχνος, ον – compassionate	ὀσμή, ῆς, ἡ – fragrance
εὐωδία, ας, ἡ – sweet smell, fragrance	παροργισμός, οῦ, ὁ – anger
θυμός, οῦ, ὁ – rage	πικρία, ας, ἡ – bitterness
θυσία, ας, ἡ – sacrifice	πλησίος, α, ον – near, neighbor
κακία, ας, ἡ – evil	προσφορά, ᾶς, ἡ – offering
κλέπτω – I steal	σαπρός, ά, όν – bad, rotten
κοπιάω – I work	σφραγίζω – I seal
κραυγή, ῆς, ἡ – yelling	χαρίζομαι – I forgive
λυπέω – I grieve	χρηστός, ή, όν – kind
μεταδίδωμι – I give	ψεῦδος, ους, τό – lie, falsehood

This unit unpacks the previous one, moving again from *is* to *ought* (see notes at 4:1).[1] A new identity in Christ and way of thinking by the Spirit lead to a different way of life. Rhetorically, Paul employs a shotgun blast of commands—eleven explicit occurrences of the imperative, but also several implied commands. The **present imperative tense** forms suggest general, open-ended commands.[2] Several also take the form of litotes, beginning with a negative formulation to emphasize the positive command ("do not steal, but give").

---

[1] If the opening διό is not original (see below), it is better classified as a subunit. See Richard M. Cozart, *This Present Triumph: An Investigation into the Significance of the Promise of a New Exodus of Israel in the Letter to the Ephesians* (Eugene, OR: Wipf & Stock, 2013), 192.

[2] Aorist imperatives are often specific commands.

4:25–5:2—RULES FOR NEW LIFE

²⁵ Διὸ³ ἀποθέμενοι⁴ τὸ ψεῦδος **λαλεῖτε ἀλήθειαν ἕκαστος μετὰ τοῦ πλησίον αὐτοῦ**, ὅτι ἐσμὲν ἀλλήλων μέλη.⁵ [Zech 8:16]

ἀποθέμενοι (ἀποτίθημι) – The repetition latches this unit to the previous (v. 22).

τὸ ψεῦδος – The arthrous substantive τὸ ψεῦδος suggests a particular lie—the deceitful lusts corrupting the old person (v. 22).

ἀλήθειαν – The importance of truth has recently been affirmed in context. This may allude to the occurrence at v. 21, which is also anarthrous, or it may have here an adverbial (degree) function: "speak truthfully" (NIV). In any case, truth is available to all in Jesus, the members of Christ's body. There is room in Ephesians for teachers (4:11) and communal edification (5:18–21).

μέλη – The body "members" presupposes the headship (κεφαλή) of Christ.

²⁶ **ὀργίζεσθε⁶ καὶ μὴ ἁμαρτάνετε·** ὁ ἥλιος μὴ ἐπιδυέτω ἐπὶ παροργισμῷ⁷ ὑμῶν, ²⁷ μηδὲ δίδοτε τόπον τῷ διαβόλῳ. [Ps 4:5 OG]

Paul cites two Scriptures, but without citation formulas. This may de-emphasize the **intertextuality**, i.e., the meaning that results from reading one text as an extension of another. The first text is from the prophet Zechariah (8:16), the only instance in the Pauline corpus. In both contexts, the writer sketches a before-and-after picture in light of God's activity.⁸ The prophet anticipates the end of exile/new exodus. Paul writes from the perspective of fulfillment and with a more inclusive understanding of neighbor. The second text is from Psalm 4 (v. 5 OG). This would be the only citation in the NT, although Paul cites the Psalter twice earlier (1:22// Ps 8:7; 4:8 // Ps 68:19).⁹ In the original context, David appears to encourage anger, but to take the emotion to God. The crisis resolves with an exhortation to "offer right sacrifices" and "trust in the Lord" (v. 6 OG).

---

³ P⁴⁶ omits Διό. However, the inferential conjunction marks a shift from the previous unit (Larkin, *Ephesians*, 97).

⁴ The syntax is probably causal (Wallace, *Greek Grammar*, 605). Some view this as an example of attendant circumstance, but λαλεῖτε is in the present tense form (Larkin, *Ephesians*, 97). The middle voice focuses on the actor of the action—in this case, the act of laying aside the lie, which enslaves the old person (see below and v. 22).

⁵ A less frequent pattern of the third declension neuter. The stem of μέλος is actually μέλες. The sigma drops out, which creates a contraction in the genitive singular (μέλους). The same occurs in the nominative/accusative plural form μέλη.

⁶ Some claim an implicit conditional or concessive sense: "if you get angry…" (Larkin, *Ephesians*, 98). At one time, the verb would have been classified as "deponent" in the present tense, but should be treated as a middle, which fits the self-involvement of the action.

⁷ The substantive may have been originally arthrous. The article (τῷ) is absent in some early, important witnesses (P⁴⁹, the original wording of Cod.Sinai, Cod.Alex, and Cod.Vat). It is witnessed to by Cod.Bezae, an editor of Cod.Sinai, and Byz mss. It is difficult to understand why the article would be added. Paul usually has an article to fill the slot of the possessive pronoun.

⁸ Cozart, *This Present Triumph*, 193.

⁹ Larkin claim this is not a citation because it lacks an introductory formula (*Ephesians*, 98).

ὀργίζεσθε καὶ μὴ ἁμαρτάνετε – The legitimacy of the so-called **adversative καί** is debated.[10] Some claim καί essentially coordinates elements, allowing only "and" or "also" as translations.[11] But others look to context for the occasional adversative sense. Here, it seems more logical for Paul to say, "Be angry, *and yet* do not sin," with all the dangers involved with this response to sin. BDAG allows "emphasizing a fact as surprising or unexpected or noteworthy: *and yet*."[12]

Many interpret this exhortation in a general sense: anger is inevitable, but do not allow it to stew. However, the plural verbs and context suggest a communal reading. Wallace alternatively claims the issue is church discipline.[13] He observes that παροργισμός "is used almost exclusively of the source of anger, not the result. That is, it refers to an external cause or provocation, not an internal reaction."[14] Paul described non-believers as "children of wrath" (2:3). Perhaps the church has been given authority to administer wrath. The Father disciplines all his children (Heb 12:1–11). But those who remain unrepentant, even after the threefold sequence of church discipline (Matt 18:15–20), must be quickly removed to protect the moral purity of the community—lest all the dough is leavened (1 Cor 5:1–13). To do otherwise gives "a place to the devil."[15] "Be angry," then, is not concessive, but a true command: the church *should* get angry about sin and deal with it, but not become compromised in the process.

28 ὁ κλέπτων μηκέτι κλεπτέτω, μᾶλλον δὲ κοπιάτω ἐργαζόμενος ταῖς[16] ἰδίαις[17] χερσὶν τὸ ἀγαθόν,[18] ἵνα ἔχῃ μεταδιδόναι τῷ χρείαν ἔχοντι.

ἐργαζόμενος ταῖς ἰδίαις χερσὶν τὸ ἀγαθόν – This echoes ἐπὶ ἔργοις ἀγαθοῖς of 2:10. The middle voice verb ἐργαζόμενος focuses on the actor—here, the self-involved act of laboring.

χερσίν – This is an excellent example of a dative of means.

---

[10] See John DelHousaye, review of Mikeal C. Parsons, Martin M. Culy, and Joshua J. Stigall, *Luke: A Handbook on the Greek Text*, *Review of Biblical Literature* [http://www.bookreviews.org] (2012).

[11] Black, *Sentence Conjunctions*, 138.

[12] The entry for καί in BDAG is remarkable exhaustive and worth careful reading.

[13] *Greek Grammar*, 492.

[14] *Greek Grammar*, 113.

[15] When Paul practices church discipline he "delivers" the unrepentant "over to Satan" (1 Cor 5:5; 1 Tim 1:20).

[16] Instrumental, modifying a middle voice participle.

[17] Omitted in P[46] and probably P[49], as well as Cod.Vat. A few mss also omit ἰδίαις, and read: τὸ ἀγαθόν ταῖς χερσίν, "[what is] useful with hands." Miniscule 629 and a few other witnesses read αὐτοῦ instead of ἰδίαις within a prepositional phrase: ἐν ταῖς χερσὶν αὐτοῦ τὸ ἀγαθόν. Miniscule 1505 and a few other witnesses include ἰδίαις with the alternate order: τὸ ἀγαθόν ταῖς ἰδίαις χερσίν, "[what is] useful with (their) own hands." The reading is not significant because the sense is implicit in the context. We follow the fuller, original wording of Cod.Sinai along with Cod.Bezae and other mss. We find this wording elsewhere in the *corpus Paulinum* (1 Cor 4:12). 1 Thess 4:11 has the same textual problem.

[18] A few later witnesses only read τὸ ἀγαθόν after ἐργαζόμενος—a simplifying edit. The absence of τὸ ἀγαθόν may be explained by the potential of the verb being intransitive as we find with the otherwise parallel expressions in the *corpus Paulinum* (1 Cor 4:12; 1 Thess 2:9; 4:12). Yet Paul uses τὸ ἀγαθόν with the verb (Gal 6:10; Rom 2:10).

²⁹ πᾶς λόγος σαπρὸς ἐκ τοῦ στόματος ὑμῶν μὴ ἐκπορευέσθω, ἀλλὰ εἴ¹⁹ τις ἀγαθὸς²⁰ πρὸς οἰκοδομὴν τῆς χρείας²¹, ἵνα δῷ χάριν τοῖς ἀκούουσιν.

λόγος – Here λόγος probably has the sense of "message" or "sermon" (1:13).

χρείας (from χρεία, ἡ) – the immediate repetition (see v. 28) latches with the preceding exhortation, perhaps highlighting material and spiritual needs.

σαπρός – The adjective σαπρός,-ά,-όν is related to the verb σήπω "make putrid"; the image is probably of spoiled food like fish or fruit.²² The saying may echo Jesus:

> Be careful because of false prophets who come to you in clothing of sheep but inwardly are hungry wolves. Because of their fruits you will know them. Do they gather grape-clusters from thorn bushes or figs from thistles? Likewise, any good tree yields good fruits, but the worthless [σαπρός] tree yields bad fruits. A good tree is not able to yield bad fruits, nor is a bad tree able to yield good fruits. Any tree which does not yield good fruit is chopped down and cast into fire. So indeed because of their fruits you will know them. (Matt 7:15–20)²³

³⁰ καὶ μὴ λυπεῖτε τὸ πνεῦμα τὸ ἅγιον²⁴ τοῦ θεοῦ, ἐν ᾧ ἐσφραγίσθητε εἰς ἡμέραν ἀπολυτρώσεως.

μή – The omission of μή in P⁴⁶ is humorous ("Grieve the Holy Spirit!") and a classic example of **Codices recentiores—non deteriores**, "later manuscripts, but not inferior."²⁵

³¹ πᾶσα πικρία καὶ θυμὸς καὶ ὀργὴ καὶ κραυγὴ καὶ βλασφημία ἀρθήτω ἀφ᾽ ὑμῶν σὺν πάσῃ κακίᾳ.

πᾶσα πικρία – This adjective is congruent with πικρία, but may indirectly modify all the substantives, which emphasize bad speech. πικρία continues the bad food theme, and may also connote harsh speech (Rom 3:14). θυμός describes rage. κραυγή may signify a loud argument and loss of order (Acts 23:9). βλασφημία is speech that denigrates or defames.

ὀργή – This noun is interesting because of its cognate imperative at v. 26. Does Paul intend a semantic shift—a different meaning for anger? Perhaps this list is the very danger that concerned the apostle: be angry, but do not allow it to degenerate into communal discord.

ἀρθήτω (from αἴρω) – The aorist tense form breaks with the other imperatives in the unit. This suggests a particular, possibly decisive command to remove these vices once and for all.

---

¹⁹ Introduces an elided first class conditional protasis (Larkin, *Ephesians*, 102).

²⁰ Repetition from v. 28.

²¹ Some mss read πίστεως for χρείας. This appears to result from some dissatisfaction with the more difficult reading. χρείας serves rhetorically as a linking repetition of v. 28. The genitive has been taken as objective, content, quality, and reference (Larkin, *Ephesians*, 102).

²² See Matt 7:17; 13:48 and BDAG for references in Greek literature.

²³ My translation.

²⁴ The restrictive attributive position emphasizes "Holy."

²⁵ See G. Pasqueli, *Storia della tradizione e critica del testo*, 2nd ed. (Florence: Olscchky, 1971), 43–108.

32 γίνεσθε²⁶ εἰς ἀλλήλους χρηστοί, εὔσπλαγχνοι, χαριζόμενοι ἑαυτοῖς²⁷ καθὼς καὶ ὁ θεὸς ἐν Χριστῷ ἐχαρίσατο ὑμῖν.²⁸

χρηστοί – The adjective χρηστός,-ή,-όν, "easy," "fine," "kind," was a favorite pun in the early church for Χριστός. Chapter 4 ends with a twofold character assessment of Christ like its opening: χρηστοί and εὔσπλαγχνοι. Langton's chapter division is therefore justified.

εὔσπλαγχνοι – The two termination adjective εὔσπλαγχνος,-ον, "compassionate," may evoke the Jesus tradition; see the cognate verb σπλαγχνίζομαι at, e.g., Mark 6:34; 8:2; Matt 9:36.

5.1 γίνεσθε οὖν μιμηταὶ τοῦ θεοῦ, ὡς τέκνα ἀγαπητά, ²καὶ περιπατεῖτε ἐν ἀγάπῃ, καθὼς καὶ ὁ Χριστὸς ἠγάπησεν²⁹ ἡμᾶς³⁰ καὶ παρέδωκεν ἑαυτὸν³¹ ὑπὲρ ἡμῶν³² προσφορὰν³³ καὶ θυσίαν τῷ θεῷ εἰς ὀσμὴν εὐωδίας.

οὖν – The inferential οὖν fits the context where Paul focuses on the kindness and grace of God (v. 32). We imitate God by following Christ's self-sacrificial example. The present imperative περιπατεῖτε encodes imperfective aspect, suggesting an ongoing way of life (see 4:1). ἐν ἀγάπῃ is adverbial, explaining *how* to walk.

ὡς τέκνα ἀγαπητά – This descriptor for believers echoes how Christ is described in 1:6.

ὁ Χριστὸς ἠγάπησεν ἡμᾶς καὶ παρέδωκεν ἑαυτὸν – This is a fairly clear example of the epexegetical καί.

προσφορὰν καὶ θυσίαν –These two nouns are a hendiadys "offering of sacrifice" (Ps 39:7OG; 1 Esdr 5.51; *Odes* 7.38; Sir 34.19). προσφορά emphasizes the action of the one offering the sacrifice; θυσία, the object. We may also speak of subjective and objective emphases. Jesus's work on the cross encompasses both since he is both agent and object.

---

²⁶ P⁴⁹ and Cod.Sinai read δὲ after γίνεσθε. The original hand of Cod.Bezae and a few other mss read οὖν. P⁴⁶ and Cod.Vat lack any conjunction. The shorter, more difficult reading is preferred. Scribes probably felt compelled to clarify the syntax.

²⁷ A reciprocal use of the reflexive pronoun.

²⁸ The verb involves inter-personal relations, and may take a dative for its direct object.

²⁹ The aorist tense form presumes distance between the action and observer, which allows a completed action in the past—in this case, Jesus's atoning death on the cross. These comments also apply to παρέδωκεν.

³⁰ Representatives of the Alexandrian tradition read ὑμᾶς (original hand of Cod.Sinai, Cod.Vat, and Cod.Alex). Yet the first person occurs in P⁴⁶ as well as in Byz mss.

³¹ The reflexive pronoun highlights the participation of the subject.

³² Cod.Vat reads ὑμῶν.

³³ A Double Accusative of object-complement (review week 3).

ACTIVITIES & QUESTIONS

1. Read the BDAG entry on καί. What was the most unusual gloss (translation option) for you?

2. Do you agree with Wallace's church discipline reading? Why or Why not?

3. Where else in Scripture are God's people called to "be like God"? Compare and contrast these places across Scripture with Paul's specific command and its particulars in Eph 5:1-2.

WEEK 11—EPH 5:3–21

Key Terms: *a fortiori*, polysendeton, from the abstract to the concrete, third person imperative, genitive of association, gnomic present, indirect middle, reciprocal pronoun

Vocabulary

ἀγαθωσύνη, ης, ἡ – goodness	καθεύδω – I sleep, am dead
ᾄδω – I sing	κενός, ή, όν – empty
ἀκαθαρσία, ας, ἡ – impurity	κληρονομία, ας, ἡ – inheritance
ἄκαρπος, ον – unfruitful	κρυφῇ – in secret
ἀκριβῶς – carefully	μεθύσκω – I get drunk
αἰσχρός, ά, όν – shameful	μωρολογία, ας, ἡ – foolish talk
αἰσχρότης, ητος, ἡ – obscenity	ὀνομάζω – I name
ἀνήκω – I am proper	πλεονέκτης, ου, ὁ – greedy person
ἀνίστημι – I rise	πλεονεξία, ας, ἡ – greed
ἀπατάω – I deceive	πνευματικός, ή, όν – spiritual
ἀπείθεια, ας, ἡ – disobedience	πορνεία, ας, ἡ – sexual immorality
ἄσοφος, ον – unwise	πόρνος, ου, ὁ – sexually immoral person
ἀσωτία, ας, ἡ – dissipation	ποτέ – formerly
ἄφρων, ον – foolish	πρέπω – I am fitting
δοκιμάζω – I discern	σοφός, ή, όν – wise
ἐλέγχω – I expose	συγκοινωνέω – I am connected with
εἰδωλολάτρης, ου, ὁ – idolater	συμμέτοχος, ον – participant
ἐπιφαύσκω – I shine	συνίημι – I understand
εὐάρεστος, ον – acceptable	ὕμνος, ου, ὁ – hymn
εὐτραπελία, ας, ἡ – filthy talk	ψάλλω – I make music
εὐχαριστία, ας, ἡ – thanksgiving	ψαλμός, οῦ, ὁ – psalm
ἐξαγοράζω – I make the most of	ᾠδή, ῆς, ἡ – song

The δέ anticipates the opposite of Christ's example of loving self-sacrifice, the *imitatio Dei* (5:1–2). The subsequent vices—two sets of three—describe life apart from Christ. The language echoes 4:17–19.

5:3–6—RENOUNCE PAGAN WAYS

> ³Πορνεία δὲ καὶ ἀκαθαρσία πᾶσα¹ ἢ πλεονεξία μηδὲ ὀνομαζέσθω ἐν ὑμῖν² καθὼς πρέπει ἁγίοις

Πορνεία, ἀκαθαρσία, πλεονεξία – Each describes aspects of sexual immorality: the act, effect, and cause. Πορνεία is "unlawful sexual intercourse—*prostitution, unchastity, fornication*"; ἀκαθαρσία, a state of moral corruption that, among other things, disrupts perception of the truth; πλεονεξία, a desire to have more than one's due—*greediness, insatiableness,* avarice, *covetousness.* The path goes from insatiable desire to mental corruption to immoral behavior. The language echoes 4:19 (see above).

Paul employs the rhetorical device **a fortiori** ("argument from a yet stronger reason"), also known in Hebrew as *qal vahomer.* Paul implies the argument: What is not spoken of should never be done. The embarrassment of immoral behavior results from an honor/shame culture.

ἁγίοις – With perhaps one exception (3:8, which is textually problematic), Paul uses the article with the substantive, referring to a group—*the holy ones* (1:1, 18; 2:19; 4:12). By omitting the article, he emphasizes the *quality* of holiness.

> ⁴καὶ³ αἰσχρότης καὶ⁴ μωρολογία ἢ⁵ εὐτραπελία ἃ⁶ οὐκ ἀνῆκεν⁷ ἀλλὰ μᾶλλον εὐχαριστία.⁸

Paul assumes the verb from the previous clause: "And do not let … be named."

The **polysyndeton**—i.e., the repeated conjunctions in quick succession often in lists—invited several variants (see footnotes). The effect of polysendeton sustains attention on each listed item.

αἰσχρότης, μωρολογία, εὐτραπελία—Each describes language that tarnishes the mind and heart. αἰσχρότης may be abstract for αἰσχρολογία, as the parallel in Col 3:8 suggests—speech in poor taste. μωρολογία emphasizes the stupidity (μωρός) of the language; εὐτραπελία goes in the opposite direction, stressing wit, but with a negative connotation.⁹

εὐχαριστία may refer to the Eucharist (Lord's Supper) as the verbal form at v. 20 suggests.¹⁰ If so, we may have a liturgical *inclusio* (5:1–3 // 19–20).

---

¹ Byz mss place πᾶσα before ἀκαθαρσία.

² The dative conveys association (BDAG: "should not even be mentioned among you").

³ Cod.Alex and Cod.Bezae read instead ἤ "or," a disjunctive particle.

⁴ Cod.Sinai, Cod.Alex, and Cod.Bezae read ἤ "or", a disjunctive particle.

⁵ P⁴⁶ reads καί.

⁶ Byz mss read τά. The neuter gender of the relative pronoun is initially surprising because the antecedents are feminine. This is probably a case where sense agreement supersedes syntax (*constructio ad sensum*): "things (such as these) which are unfitting."

⁷ The Byz tradition reads as a present participle: ἀνήκοντα. The imperfect ἀνῆκεν is the more difficult reading. The sense may be a customary imperfect (Wallace, *Greek Grammar,* 548).

⁸ ἀλλά often sets up ellipsis. Here, the sense is instead of speaking evil, offer prayers of thanksgiving.

⁹ BDAG s.v. εὐτραπελία

¹⁰ See 1 Cor 10:16; Ignatius *Eph.* 13:1; *Did.* 14:1; noted as a possibility by Muddiman, *Ephesians,* 233.

⁵ τοῦτο γὰρ ἴστε¹¹ γινώσκοντες¹² ὅτι πᾶς πόρνος ἢ ἀκάθαρτος ἢ πλεονέκτης, ὅ ἐστιν εἰδωλολάτρης, οὐκ ἔχει κληρονομίαν ἐν τῇ βασιλείᾳ τοῦ Χριστοῦ καὶ θεοῦ. ⁶Μηδεὶς ὑμᾶς ἀπατάτω κενοῖς λόγοις, διὰ ταῦτα γὰρ ἔρχεται ἡ ὀργὴ τοῦ θεοῦ ἐπὶ τοὺς υἱοὺς τῆς ἀπειθείας.

ἴστε – The perfect tense form ἴστε (from οἶδα) may be in the indicative or imperative mood. If imperative, the construction is something like an infinitive absolute: "knowing this, be aware." Otherwise (and more likely), it is a periphrastic perfect: "you have known this." Virtually all the standard translations follow this sense, which keeps to the letter's style. The perfect tense form emphasizes the stative quality of the verb.¹³

πόρνος ... ἀκάθαρτος ... πλεονέκτης – Paul moves **from the abstract to the concrete**, repeating several stems from v. 3: πόρνος from πορνεία; ἀκάθαρτος from ἀκαθαρσία; πλεονέκτης from πλεονεξία. Here in v. 5 the anarthrous substantives emphasize the quality of the unclean state from the immoral behavior already described in v. 3.

πόρνος – This word may signify homosexual behavior (Xenophon, *Mem.* 1.6.13; Demosthenes, *Epistle* 4:11) or even a male prostitute (for the female, see 1 Cor 6:15). But in the LXX and Paul's letters elsewhere, the term signifies generally sexual immorality vis-à-vis the Jewish purity code (Sir 23:16–18; 1 Cor 5:9–11; 6:9).

τοῦ Χριστοῦ καὶ θεοῦ – The single article suggests a close or overlapping relationship of Christ and God—probably a co-regency (see Col 1:13). A couple of later codices reverse the order, τοῦ θεοῦ καὶ Χριστοῦ, probably for theological or stylistic reasons.

διὰ ταῦτα – The unusual plural, the only occurrence in Paul's letters (cf. 1:15; 5:17; 6:13; but see 1 Esd 6:32), reflects the variegated vices above.

ἔρχεται – Perhaps a **gnomic present**: "The present tense may be used to make a statement of a general, timeless fact. It does not say that something *is* happening, but that something *does* happen." The action or state continues without time limits. The verb is used "in proverbial statements or general maxims about what occurs at *all* times."¹⁴ Yet the present tense form still conveys imperfective aspect: the writer intends for the reader to see the action in a dynamic, unfolding way.

τοὺς υἱοὺς τῆς ἀπειθείας – This phrase echoes 2:2–3.

---

¹¹ Byz mss read ἐστε.

¹² Possibly a redundant (pleonastic) participle.

¹³ Some find the aspectual force of εἰμί to be ambiguous.

¹⁴ Wallace, *Greek Grammar*, 523. Wallace applies this syntax to "instances that depict *deity or nature as the subject of the action*." See Rom 1:18.

5:7–14—BE LIGHT; DON'T PARTICIPATE IN DARKNESS

This unit recapitulates the substance of the previous one.

> [7] μὴ οὖν[15] γίνεσθε[16] συμμέτοχοι αὐτῶν· [8] ἦτε[17] γάρ ποτε σκότος, νῦν δὲ φῶς ἐν κυρίῳ· ὡς τέκνα φωτὸς περιπατεῖτε, [9] ὁ γὰρ καρπὸς τοῦ φωτὸς[18] ἐν πάσῃ ἀγαθωσύνῃ καὶ δικαιοσύνῃ καὶ ἀληθείᾳ, [10] δοκιμάζοντες τί ἐστιν εὐάρεστον τῷ κυρίῳ· [11] καὶ μὴ συγκοινωνεῖτε τοῖς ἔργοις τοῖς ἀκάρποις τοῦ σκότους, μᾶλλον δὲ καὶ ἐλέγχετε, [12] τὰ γὰρ κρυφῇ γινόμενα ὑπ᾽ αὐτῶν αἰσχρόν ἐστιν[19] καὶ λέγειν· [13] τὰ δὲ πάντα ἐλεγχόμενα ὑπὸ τοῦ φωτὸς φανεροῦται, [14] πᾶν γὰρ τὸ φανερούμενον φῶς[20] ἐστιν. διὸ λέγει· **Ἔγειρε, ὁ καθεύδων, καὶ ἀνάστα ἐκ τῶν νεκρῶν, καὶ ἐπιφαύσει σοι ὁ Χριστός.**[21]

συμμέτοχοι αὐτῶν – The pronoun conveys a **genitive of association**: "The genitive substantive indicates the one with whom the noun to which it stands related is associated."[22]

συγκοινωνεῖτε – This verb echoes the contrastingly positive association with Christ in 2:5–6.

δὲ καὶ ἐλέγχετε – In context, the verb ἐλέγχετε (from ἐλέγχω) signifies exposure and public censure. The command is probably not directed toward outsiders, but presupposes church discipline (see 4:25–27).

διὸ λέγει – Again, Paul employs this citation seen earlier in 4:8. But the reference is ambiguous. **Clement of Alexandria** presumes it is a saying of the Lord (*Protr.* 9.84.2). He quotes the subsequent line: "The sun of resurrection, begotten before the day star, who has given life with his own beams" (see 2 Pet 1:19). So the translation would be "he says . . . " (see 4:8). **Epiphanius** claims the saying comes from the *Apocalypse of Elijah* (*Haer.* 42.12.3), which may now be in the *Pseudepigrapha*, but our extant version lacks the line.[23]

σοι – This dative pronoun is usually translated "on you" (ESV, NIV, NAS), but "in you" is possible.

ἐπιφαύσει σοι ὁ Χριστός – Instead of this reading, Cod.Bezae offers a fascinating variant: "you will touch Christ" (ἐπιψαύσεις τοῦ Χριστοῦ).

---

[15] οὖν marks out a new (sub)unit (Hoehner, *Ephesians*, 668).

[16] Possibly, an ingressive-progressive sense—to begin and continue (Wallace, *Greek Grammar*, 721). See 5:1. I do not see the ingressive element.

[17] The imperfect tense form allows a habitual *Aktionsart* in the past.

[18] Byz mss read πνεύματος.

[19] Neuter plural subjects take a singular verb.

[20] The anarthrous substantive may emphasize the quality of light.

[21] The article may particularize Christ ("the Christ" = Messiah).

[22] Wallace, *Greek Grammar*, 128. He notes, "The head noun to which this kind of genitival use is connected is normally prefixed with συν-."

[23] James Charlesworth, ed., *The Old Testament Pseudepigrapha*, 2 vols. (NY: Doubleday, 1985), 2:721–53.

5:15–21—BE FILLED WITH THE SPIRIT

> [15] Βλέπετε[24] οὖν ἀκριβῶς πῶς[25] περιπατεῖτε, μὴ ὡς ἄσοφοι ἀλλ᾽ ὡς σοφοί, [16] ἐξαγοραζ-όμενοι τὸν καιρόν, ὅτι αἱ ἡμέραι πονηραί εἰσιν.

οὖν – This conjunction signals an inference (see 5:1).

ἐξαγοραζόμενοι – The adverbial participle conveys means[26] or manner.[27] This is an **indirect middle**: "The subject acts *for* (or sometimes *by*) himself or herself, or in his or her *own interest*. The subject thus shows a special interest in the action of the verb."[28] Larkin suggests "buy up the time for yourself."[29]

The language echoes the Sermon on the Mount, particularly the middle section (Matt 6:1, 34).

> [17] διὰ τοῦτο μὴ γίνεσθε[30] ἄφρονες, ἀλλὰ[31] συνίετε[32] τί τὸ θέλημα[33] τοῦ κυρίου[34] [18] καὶ μὴ μεθύσκεσθε[35] οἴνῳ, ἐν ᾧ ἐστιν ἀσωτία, ἀλλὰ πληροῦσθε ἐν πνεύματι, [19] λαλοῦντες ἑαυτοῖς ψαλμοῖς[36] καὶ ὕμνοις καὶ ᾠδαῖς πνευματικαῖς[37], ᾄδοντες καὶ ψάλλοντες τῇ καρδίᾳ ὑμῶν τῷ κυρίῳ, [20] εὐχαριστοῦντες πάντοτε ὑπὲρ πάντων ἐν ὀνόματι τοῦ κυρίου ἡμῶν Ἰησοῦ Χριστοῦ τῷ θεῷ καὶ πατρί,[38] [21] ὑποτασσόμενοι ἀλλήλοις ἐν φόβῳ Χριστοῦ.[39]

πληροῦσθε ἐν πνεύματι – There are several interpretations of the syntax: agency (assuming an

---

[24] The present tense form suggests a general command.

[25] Cod.Bezae and Byz mss place πῶς before ἀκριβῶς. A few other mss reflect this order, but with an additional vocative at the beginning (Cod.Alex and an editor of Cod.Sinai). Most translations (NASB, NRSV, ESV) have the adverb modify Βλέπετε. Yet if this alternative order is preferred, ἀκριβῶς is more likely modifying περιπατεῖτε: "Watch that you walk carefully"; see Hoehner, *Ephesians*, 691.

[26] Larkin, *Ephesians*, 122.

[27] Hoehner, *Ephesians*, 692.

[28] Wallace, *Greek Grammar*, 419.

[29] *Ephesians*, 122.

[30] An "ingressive-progressive action" (Hoehner, *Ephesians*, 696).

[31] Strong adversative.

[32] Several mss read as a present active participle.

[33] The original reading of Cod.Sinai was φρόνημα ("mindset").

[34] Cod.Alex and several Byz mss read θεοῦ; P[46] reads χριστοῦ.

[35] Traditional deponent, taken as a middle: "get drunk" (NET).

[36] P[46] and Cod.Vat read ἐν ψαλμοῖς. The early reading is impressive. In the Koine period, prepositions were added in a way that older Greek speakers may have found to be redundant, as in this case where the dative can convey means by itself. We cannot be certain, but it is probably more likely that a scribe added the preposition for clarity. The shorter, more difficult reading is preferred. The sense is hardly affected.

[37] The adjective may modify ᾠδαῖς or, according to Larkin, all three substantives, including ψαλμοῖς and ὕμνοις (*Ephesians and Colossians*, 126). The other terms are masculine. Faced with the diversity, Paul may have adopted the genre of nearest. However, the parallel in Colossians suggests stereotypical language. "Spiritual songs" is more appropriate.

[38] A Granville Sharp personal construction (see 1:3; Wallace, *Greek Grammar*, 274).

[39] Some would place v. 21 in the following unit, the household code (see NRSV; Talbert, *Ephesians and Colossians*, 130–31).

inter-personal relationship), means/instrumental,[40] or spatial/sphere.[41] The phrase does not technically express the content of filling, which makes the translation "filled with the Spirit" problematic. In my opinion, the content is the full and fulfilling body of Christ (1:23).

λαλοῦντες – This and the subsequent participles ᾄδοντες, ψάλλοντες, εὐχαριστοῦντες may convey means or, more likely, result.[42] Talbert argues the participle gives a "consequence" of being filled in the Spirit.[43] Although the participles are in the present tense form, according to Wallace, subsequent action is intended.[44] Perhaps.

ὑποτασσόμενοι – Some attempt to read this participle imperatively, largely because of the subsequent clause, which lacks an imperative in several mss. Yet there is no decisive reason to isolate it from the previous four participles, modifying πληροῦσθε.[45] The voice may be passive or middle. BDAG offers this entry for **ὑποτάσσω**:

ὑποτάσσω 1 aor. ὑπέταξα. Pass.: 2 fut. ὑποταγήσομαι; 2 aor. ὑπετάγην; perf. ὑποτέταγμαι (Aristot., Polyb.+)

1. to cause to be in a submissive relationship, *to subject, to subordinate*

a. act., abs. **Ro 8:20b;** 1 Cl 2:1b. τινά *bring someone to subjection* (Herodian 7, 2, 9) IPol 2:1. τινί τινα or τι *someone* or *someth. to someone* (Epict. 4, 12, 12 of God ὑπ. τί τινι; cp. Da 11:39 Theod.; TestJud 21:2; ApcSed 6:2; SibOr fgm. 3, 12; Ar. [Milne 76, 49]; Menander Eph.: 783 fgm. 1, 119 Jac. [in Jos., C. Ap. 1, 119]; Just., A I, 49, 7, A II 5, 2.—Cp. ὑπέταξεν ἑαυτοῦ τῇ ἐξουσίᾳ τοὺς Πάρθους Hippol., Ref. 9, 16, 4) **1 Cor 15:27c, 28c; Phil 3:21; Hb 2:5, 8b;** Dg 10:2; Hm 12, 4, 2; AcPl Ha 8, 15. In the same sense ὑπ. τι ὑπὸ τοὺς πόδας τινός **1 Cor 15:27a; Eph 1:22;** also ὑποκάτω τῶν ποδῶν τινος **Hb 2:8a** (Ps 8:7). ὑποτάσσειν ἑαυτόν τινι *subject oneself to someone* (Plut., Mor. 142e to the husband; Simplicius In Epict. p. 33 Düb. to transcendent powers) Hs 9, 22, 3.

b. pass.

α. *become subject* τινί to a pers. or a state of being (Iren. 5, 5, 2 [Harv. II 332, 11]) **Ro 8:20a; 1 Cor 15:28a; Hb 2:8c; 1 Pt 3:22;** Dg 7:2; Pol 2:1. Abs. (Diod. S. 1, 55, 10; Aristobulus in Eus., PE 8, 10, 10 [=p. 140 Holladay] πάνθ' ὑποτέτακται; Just., D. 85, 2 νικᾶται καὶ ὑποτάσσεται [Ath. 18, 2]; Iren. 1, 13, 4 [Harv. I 120, 7]) **1 Cor 15:27b.**

β. *subject oneself, be subjected* or *subordinated, obey* abs. (Jos., Bell. 4, 175) **Ro 13:5; 1 Cor 14:34** (cp. δουλεύετε ἀλλήλοις Gal 5:13); 1 Cl 2:1a; 57:2. Of submission involving

---

[40] Wallace, *Greek Grammar*, 170–71, 375; Larkin, *Ephesians,* 124–25.
[41] John Paul Heil, "Ephesians 5:18b: 'But Be Filled in the Spirit,'" *CBQ* 69 (2007): 506–16.
[42] Wallace, *Greek Grammar*, 351; Larkin, *Ephesians,* 124.
[43] *Ephesians and Colossians,* 130.
[44] *Greek Grammar,* 623–27.
[45] Wallace, *Greek Grammar,* 651–52; Hoehner, *Ephesians,* 716; Talbert, *Ephesians and Colossians,* 131.

recognition of an ordered structure, w. dat. of the entity to whom/which appropriate respect is shown (Palaeph. 38 p. 56, 15; 57, 2): toward a husband (s. Ps.-Callisth. 1, 22, 4 πρέπον ἐστὶ τὴν γυναῖκα τῷ ἀνδρὶ ὑποτάσσεσθαι, s. 1a above; cp. SEG 26, 1717, 26 [III/IV AD] in a love charm) **Eph 5:22 v.l.; Col 3:18; Tit 2:5; 1 Pt 3:1** (on an alleged impv. sense s. Schwyzer II 407), **5;** parents **Lk 2:51;** masters **Tit 2:9; 1 Pt 2:18;** B 19:7; D 4:11; secular authorities (1 Ch 29:24; Theoph. Ant. 1, 11 [p. 82, 14]) **Ro 13:1** (CMorrison, The Powers That Be—Ro 13:1–13, diss. Basel '56; EBarnikol, TU 77, '61, 65–133 [non-Pauline]); **Tit 3:1; 1 Pt 2:13;** 1 Cl 61:1; church officials 1 Cl 1:3; 57:1; IEph 2:2; IMg 2; 13:2; ITr 2:1f; 13:2; IPol 6:1; Pol 5:3; νεώτεροι ὑποτάγητε πρεσβυτέροις **1 Pt 5:5.** To God (Epict. 3, 24, 65 τ. θεῷ ὑποτεταγμένος; 4, 12, 11; Ps 61:2; 2 Macc 9:12) **1 Cor 15:28b; Hb 12:9; Js 4:7;** 1 Cl 20:1; IEph 5:3; to Christ **Eph 5:24.** To the will of God, the law, etc. **Ro 8:7; 10:3;** 1 Cl 34:5; Hm 12, 5, 1; τῇ ἐπιθυμίᾳ τῇ ἀγαθῇ 12, 2, 5.—Of submission in the sense of voluntary yielding in love **1 Cor 16:16; Eph 5:21; 1 Pt 5:5b v.l.;** 1 Cl 38:1.—The evil spirits must be subject to the disciples whom Jesus sends out **Lk 10:17, 20.** Likew. the prophetic spirits must be subject to the prophets in whom they dwell **1 Cor 14:32.**—HMerklein, Studien zu Jesus und Paulus (WUNT 105) '98, 405–37.

2. to add a document at the end of another document, *attach, append, subjoin* (common in official documents, hence oft. ins, pap; also s. Jos., Vi. 364, Ant. 16, 161; Just., A I, 68, 4; Mel., HE 4, 26, 14) the letters of Ign. ὑποτεταγμέναι εἰσὶν τῇ ἐπιστολῇ ταύτῃ Pol 13:2.—M-M. EDNT. TW. Spicq.

Of special note is the highly contextualized sense "of submission in the sense of voluntary yielding in love."

ἀλλήλοις – This is a **reciprocal pronoun** (ἀλλήλων). It only occurs in the genitive, dative, and accusative plural because there must be two or more people involved. BDAG offers the following translation options: "*each other, one another*, mutually." Egalitarians interpret this as a call to mutual submission in marriage (see below). F. F. Bruce notes that submissiveness is not reciprocated by husbands, parents, and masters.[46] Alan Padgett suggests it is implied.[47]

---

[46] *The Epistles to the Colossians, to Philemon, and to the Ephesians* (Grand Rapids: Eerdmans, 1984), 383.

[47] *As Christ Submits to the Church: A Biblical Understanding of Leadership and Mutual Submission* (Grand Rapids: Baker Academic, 2011), 60. See vv. 21, 25, 28, 33.

ACTIVITIES & QUESTIONS

1. In 5:3–5 Paul describes vices and lists people identified by their vices who are forfeiting their inheritance in Christ. Compare with the list in 1 Cor 6:9-10, etc. What are differences and similarities?

2. In 5:6, what are the implications of reading ἔρχεται as a gnomic present? People may avoid sin because of future consequences, like not inheriting the Kingdom or "getting caught," but what are the immediate consequences?

3. How does Paul's description here on being filled the with Spirit compare with 1 Cor 12-14?

4. What does it mean to "rebuke" or "refute" the darkness? How have followers of Christ today done this well or not done this well?

5. Should we read ὑποτασσόμενοι as an indirect middle? What are the implications of this reading? Are there disadvantages to autonomous freedom and advantages to submission?

Key Terms: household code, generic article, genitive of subordination, imperatival future

Vocabulary

ἁγιάζω – I cleanse	λουτρόν, οῦ, τό – washing
ἄμωμος, ον – unblemished, blameless	μυστήριον, ου, τό – mystery
ἀντί – because of	ποτέ – ever
ἐκτρέφω – I feed	προσκολλάω – I am united
ἔνδοξος, ον – glorious	ῥυτίς, ίδος, ἡ – wrinkle
θάλπω – I take care of	σπίλος, ου, ὁ – stain, blemish
καταλείπω – I leave	σωτήρ, ῆρος, ὁ – savior

5:22–6:9—The Christian Household

This section, broadly speaking, may be called a **household code** (German *Haustafel*); it reviews the responsibilities of spouses, children, and domestic slaves. The German *Haustafel* is attributed to Martin Luther, although the form may have a Stoic or Aristotelian provenance ("household management").[1] As the basic social unit, an ordered family was essential for communal peace—indeed, for the entire Roman Empire (*pax Romana*). This responsibility fell to the "head" of the household, the *pater familias*.

Presumably, Paul's readers would not have been surprised by much of the very standard instruction, but the genre has been infused with the humility, long-suffering, and gentleness of Christ (4:1–2). Indeed, Christ is the head of the *pater familias* in all these relations, so that imitation is expected.

Depending on what is emphasized, the unit may be read conservatively or radically. On the one hand, Southern pastors used the literal sense of the passage to defend slavery before the Civil War.[2] On the other, Stephen Fowl claims, "The role of Christian households, then, is not to imitate the predominate cultural ordering (pater familias, men, women, slaves) but to enact a counterexample."[3] The greatest revision concerns believers' marriage, which Paul interprets as a reflection of Christ's relationship with the church. Husbands had a priestly role in Jewish and Roman religion. The obedient *pater familias* became an ideal elder (1 Tim 3:4–5). I treat each group as a sub unit.

---

[1] See, for example, David E. Aune, *The New Testament in Its Literary Environment*, LEC 8 (Philadelphia: Westminster, 1987), 169.

[2] Timothy L. Wesley, *The Politics of Faith During The Civil War* (Baton Rouge, LA: Louisiana State University Press, 2013), 8–10.

[3] *Ephesians: Being a Christian at Home and in the Cosmos* (Sheffield: Sheffield Phoenix, 2014), 43.

5:22–33—WIVES & HUSBANDS

The unit is framed by exhortations to the wives—γυναῖκες (v. 22) and γυνή (v. 33). The ellipsis of the verb ὑποτάσσω and lack of a transition particle closely associates the section with what precedes.

> ^{22} Αἱ γυναῖκες τοῖς ἰδίοις ἀνδράσιν ὡς τῷ κυρίῳ, ^{23} ὅτι ἀνήρ ἐστιν κεφαλὴ τῆς γυναικὸς ὡς καὶ ὁ Χριστὸς κεφαλὴ τῆς ἐκκλησίας, ⸀αὐτὸς σωτὴρ^4 τοῦ σώματος. ^{24} ἀλλὰ^5 ⸀ὡς^6 ἡ ἐκκλησία ὑποτάσσεται τῷ Χριστῷ, οὕτως καὶ αἱ γυναῖκες ⸀τοῖς ἀνδράσιν^7 ἐν παντί.

Some later mss add the verb ὑποτάσσεσθε (probably an imperative, "Submit!") in the opening line. But our earliest mss lack a verb; this more difficult reading, a kind of ellipsis, is preferred. The implied verb ὑποτάσσω occurs in the previous clause (v. 21).[8]

αἱ γυναῖκες – The **generic article** identifies "class."[9] We will see the same phenomenon with children and slaves. Most translations leave it untranslated (e.g., NIV, NAS, ESV). This is a helpful reminder that not every article in Greek requires glossing "the" to convey its sense.

ἀνήρ – The anarthrous noun may stress the quality of being a husband: as a type of ὁ Χριστός (note the identifying article), a husband is by definition the head of the wife, the type of the church.

τῆς γυναικός – a **genitive of subordination**.[10] The article probably functions as a personal possessive pronoun ("his wife"). This allows "a husband is the head over his wife."

σωτήρ ("deliverer," "savior") is applied to God the Father (Luke 1:47; 1 Tim 1:1; 2:3; Titus 1:3; 2:10; 3:4) and the Son (Luke 2:11; Phil 3:20; 2 Tim 1:10; probably Titus 2:13), as it is here.

ὑποτάσσεται – This verb form may be either passive or middle. The latter option may have a reflexive or intensive (self-beneficial) meaning: "as the church submits herself to Christ" or "as the church (happily) yields to Christ," respectively. But the verb employment in the active voice with direct object earlier suggests the passive here: "be subject to" (see 1:22).

---

[4] Byz readings add καί and the implied ἐστιν to clarify the meaning: **καὶ** αὐτὸς **ἐστιν** σωτήρ…

[5] Byz mss read Ἀλλ'.

[6] Byz mss read ὥσπερ.

[7] Byz mss modify the substantive with ἰδίοις, which clarifies the ellipsis (see v. 22), but it is probably not original. The shorter, more difficult reading is preferred.

[8] For other examples of a "linking verb" connecting two units, see 4:1, 17; 5:2, 8, and 15; 1 Cor 5:12–13; 6:2–3. The absence of a verb at the beginning of a unit also has parallels (Rom 12:9a; 2 Cor 8:16; Col 4:6; Talbert, *Ephesians and Colossians*, 131).

[9] Wallace, *Greek Grammar*, 227–31.

[10] Larkin, *Ephesians*, 132.

²⁵ Οἱ¹¹ ἄνδρες, ἀγαπᾶτε¹² τὰς ⸀γυναῖκας,¹³ καθὼς καὶ ὁ Χριστὸς ἠγάπησεν τὴν ἐκκλησίαν καὶ ἑαυτὸν παρέδωκεν ὑπὲρ αὐτῆς, ²⁶ ἵνα αὐτὴν ἁγιάσῃ καθαρίσας¹⁴ τῷ λουτρῷ¹⁵ τοῦ ὕδατος ἐν ῥήματι, ²⁷ ἵνα παραστήσῃ ⸀αὐτὸς ἑαυτῷ¹⁶ ἔνδοξον¹⁷ τὴν ἐκκλησίαν, μὴ ἔχουσαν σπίλον ἢ ῥυτίδα ἤ τι τῶν τοιούτων, ἀλλ᾽ ἵνα ᾖ ἁγία καὶ ἄμωμος.¹⁸

ἀγαπᾶτε, ὁ Χριστὸς ἠγάπησεν, ἑαυτὸν παρέδωκεν ὑπὲρ αὐτῆς – This material evokes the Paul's opening exhortation to imitate God by loving as Christ did (5:1–2), which echoes the Jesus Tradition (e.g., Mark 10:35–45). As Christ's headship is leading to the peace, reconciliation, and harmony of all things (1:10; 2:15–16), so the Christian household can be a picture of this ultimate reality. This requires, above all else, humility and love.

ἐν ῥήματι – instrumental dative "by means of the word," a reference to the Holy Spirit (6:17).

ἑαυτῷ – This means "to himself" or possible "in himself" (see 1:4) because they are one flesh.

ἔνδοξος –This adjective signifies both an inward glory and an outward honor.

ἵνα ᾖ ἁγία καὶ ἄμωμος – This subordinate clauses echoes the opening benediction at 1:4.

²⁸ οὕτως ὀφείλουσιν ⸀καὶ¹⁹ οἱ ἄνδρες ἀγαπᾶν²⁰ τὰς ἑαυτῶν γυναῖκας ὡς τὰ ἑαυτῶν σώματα·²¹ ὁ ἀγαπῶν τὴν ἑαυτοῦ γυναῖκα ἑαυτὸν ἀγαπᾷ, ²⁹ οὐδεὶς γάρ ποτε τὴν ἑαυτοῦ σάρκα ἐμίσησεν, ἀλλὰ ἐκτρέφει καὶ θάλπει αὐτήν, καθὼς καὶ ὁ Χριστὸς²² τὴν ἐκκλησίαν, ³⁰ ὅτι μέλη ἐσμὲν τοῦ σώματος ⸀αὐτοῦ. ³¹ ἀντὶ τούτου καταλείψει ἄνθρωπος ⸀τὸν²³ ⸀πατέρα²⁴ καὶ ⸀τὴν²⁵ μητέρα καὶ προσκολληθήσεται²⁶ ⸀τῇ γυναικὶ⸀²⁷ αὐτοῦ, καὶ ἔσονται οἱ δύο εἰς σάρκα μίαν.

---

¹¹ A generic article.

¹² Context suggests the imperative mood.

¹³ The Byz reading ἑαυτῶν feels like a scribal clarification, appropriating the pronoun from v. 28. A few mss also read ὑμῶν. The shorter, earlier reading is preferred. The article may function as a possession pronoun.

¹⁴ The aorist participle probably conveys contemporaneous action with the subjunctive aorist tense form of the main verb. The synonymous verbs create redundancy for emphasis.

¹⁵ The dative is instrumental or possibly conveys manner. Either the water cleanses, along with the Holy Spirit (see below), or functions as a material symbol of a spiritual action.

¹⁶ Byz mss read αὐτήν. The earlier, more difficult reading is preferred. The masculine pronoun emphasizes the subject's role ("He Himself [Christ]").

¹⁷ A two-termination adjective, feminine according to context. The adjective modifies ἐκκλησίαν in the predicate position, but is fronted for emphasis (Larkin, *Ephesians*, 135).

¹⁸ A two-termination adjective, feminine according to context.

¹⁹ Absent in Byz mss.

²⁰ Byz mss read ἀγαπᾶν. Both paradigms convey the present active infinitive.

²¹ The image plays off the husband as "head."

²² Byz reads κύριος.

²³ A Byz reading.

²⁴ Byz mss modify πατέρα with αὐτοῦ.

²⁵ A Byz reading.

²⁶ The verb literally signifies "stick to" (cf. Josephus, *Ant.* 7.12.4). This is a divine passive (Mark 10:9).

²⁷ NA²⁸ reads πρὸς τὴν γυναῖκα αὐτοῦ.

After ὅτι μέλη ἐσμὲν τοῦ σώματος αὐτοῦ, an editor of Cod.Sinai and Byz mss contain a portion of Genesis 2:23: ἐκ τῆς σαρκὸς αὐτοῦ καὶ ἐκ τῶν ὀστέων αὐτοῦ. Closely following the Hebrew, the LXX (as we have it) reads: "bone from my bones and flesh from my flesh." Placing σάρξ (σαρκὸς) first fits the context, which has emphasized this part of the body (v. 29). The switch to the third person is presumably Christological. It seems unlikely to me that a scribe would express such freedom with the original wording. The citation fits Paul's rhetorical agenda.[28]

καταλείψει – The LXX and OG often translate the Hebrew with the **future**, but with an **imperatival** sense (as a command). καταλείπω in the active voice means "to leave behind"; the passive, "to remain."

The LXX (as we have it) reads: ἕνεκεν τούτου καταλείψει ἄνθρωπος τὸν πατέρα αὐτοῦ καὶ τὴν μητέρα αὐτοῦ καὶ προσκολληθήσεται πρὸς τὴν γυναῖκα αὐτοῦ καὶ ἔσονται οἱ δύο εἰς σάρκα μίαν. There are two minor differences: 1) ἕνεκεν τούτου vs. ἀντὶ τούτου (Paul); 2) the absence of personal pronouns (αὐτοῦ) after πατέρα and μητέρα (Paul).

The citation presupposes the authority of the father and mother over the son until marriage (6:1).

---

[32] τὸ μυστήριον τοῦτο μέγα ἐστίν, ἐγώ[29] δὲ λέγω εἰς Χριστὸν καὶ εἰς τὴν ἐκκλησίαν. [33] πλὴν καὶ ὑμεῖς οἱ καθ᾽ ἕνα[30] ἕκαστος τὴν ἑαυτοῦ γυναῖκα οὕτως ἀγαπάτω ὡς ἑαυτόν, ἡ δὲ γυνὴ ἵνα[31] φοβῆται[32] τὸν ἄνδρα.

πλήν – This conjunction introduces a summation "in any case."

ὑμεῖς οἱ καθ᾽ ἕνα – The article turns the prepositional phrase into an attributive adjective modifying ὑμεῖς.[33] The language individualizes the exhortation.

δέ – The δέ refocuses the discourse on the wife's household responsibility, which forms an *inclusio* with vv. 22–24.

---

[28] Peter R. Rodgers, "The Allusion to Genesis 2:23 at Ephesians 5:30," *JTS* 41 (1990): 92–94.

[29] Paul only uses ἐγώ in two other places in the letter (3:1; 4:1).

[30] οἱ καθ᾽ ἕνα: The article turns the prepositional phrase into an attributive adjective modifying ὑμεῖς (Larkin, *Ephesians,* 142).

[31] ἵνα seems to be playing off an implied verb ("I want"), and is essentially functioning as an objective clause.

[32] A present middle subjunctive: The middle voice is common with emotional states (Larkin, *Ephesians,* 143).

[33] Larkin, *Ephesians,* 142.

ACTIVITIES & QUESTIONS

1. Is Paul's teaching on marriage conservative, radical, or somewhere in between? If wives are no longer under the authority of their husbands in the broader culture, as they were in first-century Ephesus, does that impact our interpretation of this unit for the church today? How does Jesus exercise his headship over the church?

2. What do we learn about the mystery of union with Christ from this passage?

3. Should we follow Paul's interpretation of the creation story in Genesis even though it may depart from the literal sense?

WEEK 13—EPH 6:1–9

Key Terms: dative direct object, *patria potestas*, eisegesis, hendiadys, *lacuna*, antanaclasis

Vocabulary

ἀνθρωπάρεσκος, ον – people pleaser	κομίζω – I receive
ἀνίημι – I stop	μακροχρόνιος, ον – long-lived
ἀπειλή, ῆς, ἡ – threatening	νουθεσία, ας, ἡ – instruction
ἁπλότης, ητος, ἡ – sincerity	ὀφθαλμοδουλία, ας, ἡ – eye-service
γονεύς, έως, ὁ – parent	παιδεία, ας, ἡ – discipline, training
δουλεύω – I serve	παροργίζω – I am angry
ἐκτρέφω – I raise, nourish	προσωπολημψία, ας, ἡ – favoritism
ἐλεύθερος, α, ον – free	τιμάω – I honor
εὖ – well	τρόμος, ου, ὁ – trembling
εὔνοια, ας, ἡ – wholehearted	ὑπακούω – I obey

6:1–4—CHILDREN

6.1 Τὰ τέκνα, ὑπακούετε[1] τοῖς γονεῦσιν ὑμῶν ἐν κυρίῳ, τοῦτο[2] γάρ ἐστιν δίκαιον· **2 τίμα τὸν πατέρα σου καὶ τὴν μητέρα**, ἥτις[3] ἐστὶν[4] ἐντολὴ πρώτη ἐν ἐπαγγελίᾳ,[5] **3** ἵνα **εὖ σοι γένηται καὶ ἔσῃ μακροχρόνιος ἐπὶ τῆς γῆς.**

Τὰ τέκνα – The article isolates children as a class from the other groups of the *familia*.[6] The noun τέκνον (from τίκτω "engender, bear") has the core meaning of "offspring of human parents."[7] Age and gender must be determined from context. In our culture, we tend to view the obedient child as someone under the age of eighteen. We project this meaning (signified) back on the word (signifier), what some call **eisegesis** (εἰς "into" vs. ἐξηγεῖσθαι "to lead out"). In Roman society, fathers of legitimate children retained authority over them throughout life. This social reality is called ***patria potestas***. There were often five generations living in the same home. So Paul is probably instructing adult children. The obedience of small children might go without saying. The subunit is bracketed by instruction to adult wives and slaves.

---

[1] The present imperative allows a general command.

[2] The antecedent is the entire commandment. Note the neuter gender. The pronoun may also look forward to a postcedent—the Mosaic equivalent of Paul's command.

[3] The relative pronoun looks ahead to the postcedent ἐντολή.

[4] Omitted in Cod.Vat.

[5] Perhaps sphere—in the context of a biblical promise—or the thing possessed—"which possesses" (Wallace, *Greek Grammar*, 372). Manner is also possible.

[6] Wallace, *Greek Grammar*, 229.

[7] BDAG s.v. τέκνον.

τοῖς γονεῦσιν – The verb ὑπακούω may take either a genitive or **dative direct object**. The root idea of some verbs is so closely related to that of the dative, personal relation, that they take their object in that case.

ἐν κυρίῳ – The phrase is absent in Cod.Vat, the original hand of Cod.Bezae, and a few other mss. Yet textual support is early and cuts through the Alexandrian tradition (P[46], Cod.Sinai, and Cod.Alex), resting in a sea of Byz witnesses. The phrase also occurs in the Colossians parallel (3:20).[8] Except for a single occurrence in Rev 14:13, the phrase ἐν κυρίῳ is used only by Paul.[9] The object of the preposition, the Lord, forms *inclusio* around the unit (v. 4), but also anticipates the Lordship language in the instruction to slaves (vv. 5–9). Perhaps the phrase was omitted because it could imply that children were only to obey believing parents. But the more likely sense is for a child to view obedience to parents as obedience to Christ, as a wife submits to her husband (5:21).

δίκαιον – In context, the adjective refers to conformity to the Law. According to BDAG, "The neuter denotes that which is obligatory in view of certain requirements of justice, *right, fair, equitable*."[10] The "Law of Christ" does not reject lesser authorities, but realigns them under the One who sits at the right hand of the Father (1:21–22). They become accountable to his example of humility and service.

τίμα τὸν πατέρα σου καὶ τὴν μητέρα – Paul cites an ἐντολή from the Mosaic Law (Deut 5:16), presuming its continual validity (cf. Eph 2:15). Parents must teach their children to love and fear God (Deut 6:1–25). Jesus's complete obedience to his Father only deepens the commandment (Phil 2:8). The Law classifies dishonoring parents a capital offense (Deut 21:18–21). The apostle's promise, then, could be an indirect threat of losing one's life. The underlying Hebrew (ארך), which the LXX translates μακροχρόνιος "long life", may also signify "to prolong." The early church did not exercise capital punishment, but handed "people over to Satan," who presumably had been given permission by God to chasten or kill the sinful Christian. Paul assumes death for disobedience in the new covenant (1 Cor 5:5; 11:30).

ἔσῃ μακροχρόνιος ἐπὶ τῆς γῆς – The future tense allows prediction, which Paul interprets as a promise. The form differs from the LXX.[11] The subjunctive form ᾖς, to my knowledge, does not occur in the NT.

---

[8] Because of the close relationship between the letters, it may indirectly evidence originality in Ephesians. Of course, the logic may be reversed with a scribe adding the phrase to Ephesians due to memory or a desire for uniformity.

[9] Rom 14:14; 16:2, 8, 11, 12 [2x], 13, 22; 1 Cor 1:31; 4:17; 7:22, 39; 9:1, 2; 11:11; 15:58; 16:19; 2 Cor 2:12; 10:17; Gal 5:10; Eph 2:21; 4:1, 17; 5:8; 6:1, 10, 21; Phil 1:14; 2:19, 24, 29; 3:1; 4:1, 2, 4, 10; Col 3:18, 20; 4:7, 17; 1 Thess 3:8; 4:1; 5:12; 2 Thess 3:4, 12; Phm 16, 20.

[10] S.v. δίκαιον.

[11] τίμα τὸν πατέρα σου καὶ τὴν μητέρα ἵνα εὖ σοι γένηται καὶ ἵνα μακροχρόνιος γένῃ ἐπὶ τῆς γῆς τῆς ἀγαθῆς ἧς κύριος ὁ θεός σου δίδωσίν σοι (Exod 20:12); τίμα τὸν πατέρα σου καὶ τὴν μητέρα σου ὃν τρόπον ἐνετείλατό σοι κύριος ὁ θεός σου ἵνα εὖ σοι γένηται καὶ ἵνα μακροχρόνιος γένῃ ἐπὶ τῆς γῆς ἧς κύριος ὁ θεός σου δίδωσίν σοι (Deut 5:16).

⁴ Καὶ οἱ πατέρες,¹² μὴ παροργίζετε τὰ τέκνα ὑμῶν, ἀλλὰ ἐκτρέφετε αὐτὰ ἐν παιδείᾳ καὶ νουθεσίᾳ κυρίου.

Instruction to fathers takes the form of litotes: "don't do that, but do this...."

παροργίζω – "to agitate" or "anger": The verb images a father pushing his children beyond their capacity.¹³ The prefixed preposition is used with verbs of striking or wounding. In *Laws* Plato writes on effective nurture through praise rather than threats:

> He must—I mean the legislator must—commend some forms of the chase and condemn others, always with an eye on the exercises and sports of the younger men; the younger man, in his turn, must obey this advice. Neither hope of pleasure nor dread of hardship must interfere with his obedience, and he must treat the legislator's various commendations with still deeper respect and more dutiful compliance than his penalty-sanctioned ordinances. (*Leg.* 7, 823c)¹⁴

Paul reminds us that God the Father does not test beyond our capacity (1 Cor 10:13). Merciful and gracious, he allows us to grow naturally in the Trinitarian family.

ἐν παιδείᾳ καὶ νουθεσίᾳ – This prepositional phrase is a very meaningful phrase. The nouns share a close relationship—perhaps a **hendiadys**, which occurs when one idea is expressed by giving two elements as though they were independent and connecting them with a coordinating conjunction rather than subordinating one element over another ("Try and do better," not "Try to do better"; "fun and games"). This device is common in Greek literature. παιδεία is guidance for responsible living; νουθεσία, counsel about avoidance or cessation of an improper course of conduct.¹⁵

κυρίου – This may be taken as a subjective genitive—the training or discipleship by the Lord Jesus; alternatively and less directly, the genitive may indicate source.

6:5–9—SLAVES

The unit is one complex sentence (period). Paul treats slaves as part of the household, a social reality in the Mediterranean. Silences and spaces can be just as telling as words on the page—*lacuna*. In the previous relationships (wife/husband, children/parents), Paul appeals to Scripture, but not here.

---

¹² The article probably isolates fathers as a class from the other groups of the *familia* (Wallace, *Greek Grammar*, 229).

¹³ Sirach 4:3 in reference to the poor; see also Heb 12:8–10. In some witnesses, we find the same verb in the Colossian parallel (3:21). But the earlier reading is ἐρεθίζω: "to cause someone to react in a way that suggests acceptance of a challenge: (BDAG); see Comfort, *New Testament Text*, 634.

¹⁴ The translation is from Edith Hamilton and Huntington Cairns, eds., *The Collected Dialogues of Plato Including the Letters* (Princeton, NJ: Princeton University Press, 199), 1393.

¹⁵ In the two other occurrences in the *corpus Paulinum*, the term signifies a warning (1 Cor 10:11; Titus 3:10).

⁵ Οἱ¹⁶ δοῦλοι, ὑπακούετε τοῖς κατὰ σάρκα κυρίοις μετὰ φόβου καὶ τρόμου ἐν ἁπλότητι τῆς¹⁷ καρδίας ὑμῶν ὡς τῷ Χριστῷ, ⁶ μὴ κατ’ ὀφθαλμοδουλίαν ὡς ἀνθρωπάρεσκοι ἀλλ’ ὡς δοῦλοι Χριστοῦ¹⁸ ποιοῦντες¹⁹ τὸ θέλημα τοῦ θεοῦ, ἐκ ψυχῆς ⁷ μετ’ εὐνοίας δουλεύοντες²⁰, ὡς τῷ κυρίῳ καὶ οὐκ ἀνθρώποις, ⁸ εἰδότες²¹ ὅτι ἕκαστος, ὃ ἂν²² ποιήσῃ ἀγαθόν, τοῦτο²³ κομίσεται²⁴ παρὰ κυρίου,²⁵ εἴτε δοῦλος εἴτε ἐλεύθερος.

κυρίοις – Many translations render κυρίοις as "masters" (KJV, NRSV, ESV), but this undercuts the point of the word's repetition (κυρίῳ) in reference to Jesus (v. 7). Jesus, Paul reminds "lords" κατὰ σάρκα, is the ultimate head of church and family. Unless the author appropriates **antanaclasis** (ἀντανάκλασις), the repetition of a word in which a different meaning is applied, I believe we should translate the same word the same way.

μετὰ φόβου καὶ τρόμου – the hendiadys also describes our manner of service to God (Phil 2:12). The enacted humility invites divine mediation—God working through us.

ἁπλότητι – This noun ἁπλότης may refer to "generosity," but the context and core meaning suggest "focus," the opposite of a "divided mind" (δίψυχος, Jas 1:8; 4:8).²⁶ We find nearly the same wording in *Wisdom of Solomon*:

Ἀγαπήσατε δικαιοσύνην οἱ κρίνοντες τὴν γῆν φρονήσατε περὶ τοῦ κυρίου ἐν ἀγαθότητι καὶ ἐν ἁπλότητι καρδίας ζητήσατε αὐτόν,

Love righteousness, you judges of the earth, meditate on the Lord in goodness and seek him with sincerity of heart" (1:1).

The wording may have influenced the omission of the article in Cod.Sinai.

ἐκ ψυχῆς – This prepositional phrase echoes ἁπλότης.

μετ’ εὐνοίας – The noun εὔνοια "goodwill, a kindly supportive feeling" was a typical slave virtue.

---

¹⁶ The article probably isolates slaves as a class from the other groups of the *familia* (Wallace, *Greek Grammar*, 229).

¹⁷ Absent in Cod.Sinai.

¹⁸ Byz mss present the substantive as arthrous: τοῦ Χριστοῦ. This is a very common kind of expansion in the manuscript tradition.

¹⁹ The adverbial participle may convey means.

²⁰ δουλεύω takes a dative direct object.

²¹ Causal (= v. 9). Wallace notes that adverbial perfect participles are almost always causal (*Greek Grammar*, 631).

²² Byz mss add ὅ to ἐάν τι, and places the words before ἕκαστος. For the sense, see John 14:14; 1 John 5:14.

²³ The antecedent is ἀγαθόν.

²⁴ Byz mss read κομεῖται. Both spellings convey the future middle tense form: "will get back for themselves." The verb often relates to recompense.

²⁵ Byz mss present the substantive as arthrous: τοῦ κυρίου. This sort of expansion is common in the manuscript tradition.

²⁶ The former meaning has been seen in Rom 12:8 and 2 Cor 8:2; 9:11, although BDAG expresses doubt.

BDAG cites *POxy* 494, 6, the will of a certain Acusilaus (AD 156), who frees five of his slaves "according to their goodwill and affection."[27]

ἐάν τι ποιήσῃ ἀγαθόν = "whatever good each one does"

> **⁹** Καὶ οἱ[28] κύριοι, τὰ αὐτὰ ποιεῖτε πρὸς αὐτούς,[29] ἀνιέντες τὴν ἀπειλήν, εἰδότες[30] ὅτι καὶ[31] αὐτῶν καὶ ὑμῶν ὁ κύριός ἐστιν ἐν οὐρανοῖς, καὶ προσωπολημψία οὐκ ἔστιν παρ᾽ αὐτῷ.

τὰ αὐτά – This is the identical use of the personal pronoun ("the same things"), fronted here for emphasis.

ἀνιέντες – This participle is from ἀνίημι that can mean "to give up" or "cease."

αὐτῶν καὶ ὑμῶν – These fronted and emphasized genitive pronoun modifiers are absent in the Byz tradition. In agreement with the *SBLGNT* and NA[28], it is easier to see the language falling out of the manuscripts than being an earlier addition or interpolation.

ACTIVITIES & QUESTIONS

1. Should adult children be under the authority of their parents?

2. How would you integrate Paul's use of ἐντολή here with that of 2:15?

3. Is the Master/Slave relationship comparable to the Boss/Worker relationship today? What elements of this household relationship are applicable today?

---

[27] Bernard Grenfell and Arthur S. Hunt, eds., *The Oxyrhunchus Papyri, Part 3* (London: Oxford University Press, 1903), 201.

[28] The article probably isolates lords as a class from the other groups of the *familia* (Wallace, *Greek Grammar,* 229). Yet the same *pater familias* may be husband, father, and lord.

[29] Perhaps an *inclusio* with 5:21.

[30] Causal (= v.8; Wallace, *Greek Grammar,* 631).

[31] Byz mss read ὑμῶν after καί.

WEEK 14—EPH 6:10–22

Key Terms: dative of possession, *conduplicatio*, closing, epistolary aorist

Vocabulary

ἀγρυπνέω – I am alert	κοσμοκράτωρ, ορος, ὁ – world ruler
ἅλυσις, εως, ἡ – chain	κράτος, ους, τό – strength
ἀναλαμβάνω – I take up	μάχαιρα, ης, ἡ – (short) sword
ἀνθίστημι – I oppose	μεθοδεία, ας, ἡ – scheme
ἄνοιξις, εως, ἡ – opening	μυστήριον, ου, τό – mystery
ἀφθαρσία, ας, ἡ – imperishability	οἶδα – I know
βέλος, ους, τό – arrow	ὀσφῦς, ύος, ἡ – waist
γινώσκω – I know	πάλη, ης, ἡ – struggle
γνωρίζω – I make known	πανοπλία, ας, ἡ – whole armor
δέησις, εως, ἡ – petition	παρρησιάζομαι – I speak boldly
διάκονος, ου, ὁ, ἡ – servant, minister	πέμπω – I send
δίδωμι – I give	περιζώννυμι – I wrap around
ἐνδυναμόω – I become strong	περικεφαλαία, ας, ἡ – helmet
ἐνδύω – I put on	πονηρία, ας, ἡ – evil
ἐπουράνιος, ον – heavenly	πρεσβεύω – I am an ambassador
ἑτοιμασία, ας, ἡ – preparation	προσκαρτέρησις, εως, ἡ – perseverance
θυρεός, οῦ, ὁ – shield	πνευματικός, ή, όν – spiritual
θώραξ, ακος, ὁ – breastplate	πυρόω – I burn, am in flames
ἵστημι – I stand (against)	σβέννυμι – I extinguish
ἰσχύς, ύος, ἡ – might	σωτήριος, ον – brining salvation
κατεργάζομαι – I do, accomplish	ὑποδέω – I put on

6:10–17—THE WHOLE ARMOR OF GOD

This is the last unit in the body, functioning as a finale to the paranesis. It is dramatic: the Church is a Roman wedge (Latin *cuneus*), the most terrifying force in the ancient world. It was intended to "shock" and penetrate the enemy.[1] The trapezoidal formation was led front and center by a centurion. First, was the discharge of the *pila*. The lead-tipped spears weighed down the shields of the en-

---

[1] Richard A. Gabriel, *The Great Armies of Antiquity* (Westport, CT: Praeger, 2002), 270.

emy. The charge with the *gladius* followed, disemboweling the enemy.[2]

Paul uses the description to empower (vv. 10–11) and to encourage (v. 22) his readers and to remind them that they are not alone (v. 24).

Τοῦ λοιποῦ "finally" or "in sum" (see also Gal 6:17; Phil 3:1) marks the transition. The opening command echoes the opening prayer (1:19). At the end of the unit, Paul again mentions his imprisonment, forming *inclusio* with the beginning of the Paranesis (4:1).

Cutting at the Joints: It may be divided into two subunits: 1) a "nucleus" of general exhortation (vv. 10–13) and 2) "amplification" (vv. 14–20).[3]

6:10–13—The Armor of God

The subunit is delimited by the repetition of τὴν πανοπλίαν τοῦ θεοῦ, referring to both the defensive and offensive equipment of the heavily armed foot soldier.[4]

> [10] Τοῦ λοιποῦ[5] ἐνδυναμοῦσθε[6] ἐν κυρίῳ[7] καὶ ἐν τῷ κράτει τῆς ἰσχύος αὐτοῦ.[8] [11] ἐνδύσασθε[9] τὴν πανοπλίαν τοῦ θεοῦ πρὸς τὸ δύνασθαι[10] ὑμᾶς στῆναι πρὸς τὰς μεθοδείας τοῦ διαβόλου·[11] [12] ὅτι οὐκ ἔστιν ἡμῖν ἡ[12] πάλη πρὸς αἷμα καὶ σάρκα, ἀλλὰ πρὸς τὰς ἀρχάς, πρὸς τὰς ἐξουσίας, πρὸς τοὺς κοσμοκράτορας τοῦ σκότους[13] τούτου, πρὸς τὰ πνευματικὰ τῆς πονηρίας ἐν τοῖς ἐπουρανίοις. [13] διὰ τοῦτο ἀναλάβετε τὴν πανοπλίαν τοῦ θεοῦ, ἵνα δυνηθῆτε ἀντιστῆναι ἐν τῇ ἡμέρᾳ τῇ πονηρᾷ καὶ ἅπαντα κατεργασάμενοι στῆναι.

ἐνδύσασθε (from ἐνδύω) – This verb form is an aorist middle imperative. The aorist often describes specific commands; the middle voice, the reflexive act of dressing.

ἐν τῷ κράτει τῆς ἰσχύος αὐτοῦ – This prepositional phrases involves a hendiadys ("in" or "by his mighty strength"). For other possible examples, see 3:12, 17 and 6:4.

---

[2] Lindsay Powell, *Roman Soldier Vs. Germanic Warrior: 1st Century AD* (Oxford: Osprey, 2014), 19.

[3] Larkin, *Ephesians*, 155.

[4] Lincoln, *Ephesians*, 442.

[5] Τοῦ λοιποῦ is a Genitive of Reference, conveying a logical (not temporal) relationship with what precedes ("Finally"). Byz mss read ἀδελφοί μου after the adverb.

[6] The voice is passive or (reflexive) middle (with causative force): "empower yourselves" (see Larkin, *Ephesians*, 156). I favor the passive since ἐν τῷ κράτει τῆς ἰσχύος αὐτοῦ seems to convey the instrumentality of the verb.

[7] If the middle is the correct reading of the verb (see above), the dative here conveys reference or sphere.

[8] Either substantive could be the head noun, allowing either an Attributive or Attributed Genitive: "strong might" or "mighty strength." The redundancy is typical of Asiatic rhetoric. Larkin, wrongly in my opinion, treats them as reference because of his commitment to the middle voice reading of the verb (*Ephesians*, 157).

[9] The middle voice is typical for actions involving clothing.

[10] πρὸς τό + infinitive conveys purpose or result.

[11] The punctuation is too strong.

[12] Like possessive pronouns in the genitive case, the article is filling the slot for the dative ἡμῖν.

[13] Byz mss read τοῦ αἰῶνος after σκότους.

ἡμῖν – The **dative of possession** often occurs with a state-of-being (copulative) verb. Rarer than the genitive of possession, it *emphasizes the possessed object*. It is also fronted for emphasis.

αἷμα καὶ σάρκα – These together are a metonymy for a human being. The same order occurs in Hebrews 2:14, but we also find "flesh and blood" (Gal 1:16; 1 Cor 15:50; Matt 16:20; Sir 14:18; 17:31). This may reflect Lukan influence. The KJV translates "flesh and blood"; the NRSV reverted to the original order ("blood and flesh"), while the ESV switched back!

ἀλλά – This conjunction marks a litotes, emphasizing the spiritual quality of the battle.

πρός – The fivefold repetition of πρός ("against") is an expression of *conduplicatio*, the repetition of a word or phrase in more than one clause. Its purpose is "to amplify or appeal to action."[14] Moreover, each spiritual enemy is given individual weight, being arthrous: τὰς ἀρχάς, τὰς ἐξουσίας, τοὺς κοσμοκράτορας, τὰ πνευματικά.

κατεργασάμενοι (from κατεργάζομαι) – The adverbial participle may anticipate the preparation in the subsequent unit ("having done all" ESV) or denote victory: *after proving victorious over everything, to stand your ground*."[15]

μεθοδείας—See 4:14.

6:14–17—AMPLIFICATION

The subunit is marked by the inferential οὖν. The repetition of ἵστημι is a specific expression of anadiplosis, *the repetition of the last word in the previous sentence*. The device ties the subunits together, unpacking the wedge metaphor.

> [14] στῆτε[16] οὖν περιζωσάμενοι τὴν ὀσφὺν ὑμῶν ἐν ἀληθείᾳ, καὶ ἐνδυσάμενοι τὸν θώρακα τῆς δικαιοσύνης, [15] καὶ ὑποδησάμενοι τοὺς πόδας ἐν ἑτοιμασίᾳ[17] τοῦ εὐαγγελίου τῆς εἰρήνης, [16] ἐν πᾶσιν ἀναλαβόντες τὸν θυρεὸν τῆς πίστεως, ἐν ᾧ[18] δυνήσεσθε πάντα τὰ βέλη τοῦ πονηροῦ πεπυρωμένα[19] σβέσαι· [17] καὶ τὴν περικεφαλαίαν τοῦ σωτηρίου δέξασθε,[20] καὶ τὴν μάχαιραν τοῦ πνεύματος, ὅ[21] ἐστιν ῥῆμα θεοῦ,

---

[14] *Rhet. Her.* 4.28.38. See Khiok-khng Yeo, *Rhetorical Interaction in 1 Corinthians 8 & 10: A Formal Analysis with Preliminary Suggestions for a Chinese, Cross-Cultural Hermeneutic* (Leiden: Brill, 1995), 195.

[15] BDAG s.v. κατεργάζομαι; see Rom 15:18; 1 Cor 5:3.

[16] The subsequent aorist participles (περιζωσάμενοι, ἐνδυσάμενοι, ὑποδησάμενοι, ἀναλαβόντες) correlate with κατεργασάμενοι (v. 13)—modes of preparation.

[17] "Preparation," "steadfastness," or, favored by Larkin, "equipment" (*Ephesians*, 161).

[18] The antecedent of the relative pronoun is θυρεόν.

[19] Stative *Aktionsart*. The Evil One's army has lit the arrows. We find the article τά in the Byzantine tradition, which reads like a scribal improvement. It would further clarify the restrictive attributive position of the adjectival participle πεπυρωμένα. Paul may have sacrificed a bit of clarity for the euphonic alliteration.

[20] The second imperative seems to follow the first (στῆτε): "Stand … and then receive." Paul moves from defense to offense.

[21] The antecedent of the neuter pronoun would appear to be πνεύματος, not μάχαιραν. Yet some find this to

ῥῆμα θεοῦ – The anarthrous ῥῆμα emphasizes quality, a divine revelation. ὁ λόγος τοῦ θεοῦ is
more common (Rom 9:6; 1 Cor 14:36; 2 Cor 2:17; 1 Tim 4:5). This expression refers more specifically to prophecy (OG 1 Sam 9:27; 2 Kgs 14:25; 23:16; Isa 40:8; Jer 1:1). The context suggests allusion to Jesus's battle in the wilderness (Matt 4:4).

6:18–20—PRAYING IN THE HOLY SPIRIT

The two subunits are tied together with πνεῦμα (vv. 17, 18). Paul may allude to the earlier prayers
(1:3–14; 3:14–21). This is probably why he offered their contents: his audience may repeat them to
great effect.

> [18] διὰ πάσης προσευχῆς καὶ δεήσεως,[22] προσευχόμενοι ἐν παντὶ καιρῷ ἐν πνεύματι, καὶ εἰς
> αὐτὸ ἀγρυπνοῦντες ἐν πάσῃ προσκαρτερήσει καὶ δεήσει περὶ πάντων τῶν ἁγίων, [19] καὶ
> ὑπὲρ ἐμοῦ, ἵνα μοι δοθῇ λόγος ἐν ἀνοίξει τοῦ στόματός μου, ἐν παρρησίᾳ γνωρίσαι τὸ
> μυστήριον τοῦ εὐαγγελίου [20] ὑπὲρ οὗ πρεσβεύω ἐν ἁλύσει, ἵνα ἐν αὐτῷ παρρησιάσωμαι ὡς
> δεῖ με λαλῆσαι.

προσευχῆς καὶ δεήσεως – These may be hendiadys ("supplicatory prayer").

προσευχόμενοι – Many interpret the participle as imperatival (NAS, NIV, NRSV). But Wallace[23]
and Larkin[24] question this reading, seeing a continuation of the military metaphor (see KJV,
ESV). But how do we explain the transition to the present tense form, which seems to parallel
ἐνδυναμοῦσθε (v. 10), and the absence of a conjugated verb? See the transition between 5:20
and 21.

ἐν ἀνοίξει τοῦ στόματός μου – The pleonasm formalizes the discourse (Job 3:1–2; Ps 78:2).
τὸ μυστήριον – This noun echoes 3:4 and 5:32.

6:21–24—CLOSING

The **closing** is the final element of a letter.[25] Typically, this would include greetings from those
known to both sender and recipient(s) with a farewell. In the New Testament, we often find a benediction instead.

Cutting at the Joints: The unit is comprised of two subunits: 1) Sending of Tychicus and 2) Recapitulation of Salutation. At the end of the previous unit, Paul asked for prayer for his mission.

---

be non-sensical (Larkin, *Ephesians*, 162). Wallace claims the neuter comes from "attraction" to the predicate ῥῆμα
(*Greek Grammar*, 338). On the other hand, "the Spirit, who is the (spoken) word of God" is not impossible.
    [22] The dative conveys means (Hoehner, *Ephesians*, 855; Larkin, *Ephesians*, 163).
    [23] *Greek Grammar*, 163.
    [24] *Ephesians*, 163.
    [25] Porter, "A Functional Letter Perspective," 1–32.

6:21–22—SENDING OF TYCHICUS

The subunit is delimited by discussion about Tychicus. The transition is marked by δέ. The second (vv. 23–24) recapitulates Paul's prayer for peace and grace to be upon his readers, forming a final *inclusio* around the letter (1:2). Indeed, the order of peace and grace are reversed from the opening.

21 Ἵνα[26] δὲ ᾿εἰδῆτε[27] καὶ ὑμεῖς᾿ τὰ κατ᾿ ἐμέ,[28] τί πράσσω, πάντα[29] ᾿γνωρίσει ὑμῖν᾿[30] Τυχικὸς[31] ὁ ἀγαπητὸς ἀδελφὸς καὶ πιστὸς διάκονος ἐν κυρίῳ, **22** ὃν[32] ἔπεμψα πρὸς ὑμᾶς εἰς αὐτὸ τοῦτο ἵνα γνῶτε τὰ περὶ ἡμῶν καὶ παρακαλέσῃ τὰς καρδίας ὑμῶν.

ἔπεμψα – This verb is an **epistolary aorist**: the sender of the letter assumes the time frame of his readers. By the time they hear the letter read or performed (see below) by Tychichus, Paul would have sent it. Paul often employs the device (e.g., Gal 6:11; 2 Cor 8:17; Phil 2:28; Phlm 12).

παρακαλέσῃ – The verb παρακαλέω echoes the occurrence at 4:1, suggesting that Tychichus preaches Paul's sermon. In this case, the positive connotation, "to instill someone with courage or cheer, *comfort, encourage, cheer up*" (BDAG), is explicit.[33]

τὰς καρδίας ὑμῶν – This is the sixth and final occurrence of καρδία in Ephesians. The substantive has described spiritual vision (1:18) and where Christ dwells (3:17), a place of hardening (4:18), a means of sincere worship (5:19) and service (6:5). The heart is a temple.

6:23–24—RECAPITULATION OF SALUTATION

23 Εἰρήνη[34] τοῖς ἀδελφοῖς[35] καὶ ἀγάπη μετὰ πίστεως ἀπὸ θεοῦ πατρὸς καὶ κυρίου Ἰησοῦ Χριστοῦ.[36] **24** ἡ[37] χάρις[38] μετὰ πάντων τῶν ἀγαπώντων τὸν κύριον ἡμῶν Ἰησοῦν Χριστὸν ἐν ᾿ἀφθαρσίᾳ.

Asyndeton in v. 23 marks a transition to these final two verbless statements.

---

[26] The fronting of the ἵνα—but note the postpositive conjunction δέ—is unusual but not unprecedented in Paul's letters (1 Cor 16:16; 2 Cor 10:9).

[27] A "perfect" subjunctive only because of the irregular form οἶδα, which stands in the place of the obsolete εἴδω.

[28] Idiomatic expressions: "the things concerning me" or "personal matters."

[29] Here πάντα does not refer to "all things" in a universal sense, but "all things" pertaining to Paul.

[30] Byz mss place ὑμῖν before γνωρίσει.

[31] Following the Byz tradition, BDAG prefers the accent on the ultima: Τυχικός.

[32] The antecedent is Τύχικος.

[33] BDAG s.v. παρακαλέω.

[34] Εἰρήνη is fronted for emphasis. There is an understood optative verb ("be").

[35] The dative conveys advantage.

[36] Source: "Peace," "love," and "faith" or simply the latter come from (ἀπό) the Father and the Son.

[37] Since the anarthrous first occurrence of χάρις in the opening greeting (1:2), with one exception (2:5), the substantive has been arthrous, identifying the unique grace of God (1:6, 7; 2:7, 8; 3:2, 7, 8; 4:7, 29).

[38] χάρις is fronted for emphasis. There is an understood optative verb ("be").

ἐν ἀφθαρσίᾳ – This prepositional phrase probably functions adverbially ("with [love] incorrupti-ble"), explaining how we are to love Christ. The substantive occurs seven times in the NT—all in Paul's letters. BDAG offers this gloss: "the state of not being subject to de-cay/dissolution/interruption, incorruptibility, *immortality*," a sense that fits all the occurrences (Rom 2:7; 1 Cor 15:42, 50, 53, 54; 1 Tim 1:10).[39] Paul claims love never ends (1 Cor 13).

The Byzantine tradition provides a fitting ending: Ἀμήν. It is easier to explain its addition than its omission.

ACTIVITIES & QUESTIONS

1. Translations that pride themselves on being literal read "flesh and blood" (NAS, ESV). Is this a violation of their method? Would "blood and flesh" require too much processing effort for an English-speaking audience?

2. Review your text-critical work throughout Ephesians. What is your general estimation of the Byzantine tradition for recovering the original wording? Have earlier witnesses proved to be more reliable?

3. Having walked through the trees, climb a mountain to see the forest: Create your own teaching out-line for Ephesians. My divisions followed the constraints of the course—fourteen weeks. Your teaching series may be shorter or longer. Make sure to cut at the joints, so that your teaching aligns as much as possible with Paul's. Summarize the main point (exhortation) for each lesson.

---

[39] S.v. ἀφθαρσία.

BIBLIOGRAPHY

COMMENTARIES

Abbott, T. K. *A Critical and Exegetical Commentary on The Epistle to The Ephesians and The Epistle to The Colossians.* New York: Charles Scribner's Sons, 1897.

Arnold, Clinton, ed. *Ephesians: Zondervan Exegetical Commentary on the New Testament.* Grand Rapids: Zondervan, 2009.

Best, Ernest. *Ephesians.* The International Critical Commentary. Edinburgh: T&T Clark, 2001.

Bruce, F. F. *The Epistles To The Colossians, To Philemon, and To The Ephesians.* Grand Rapids: Eerdmans, 1984.

Dunn, James D. G. *The Epistles to the Colossians and to Philemon.* Grand Rapids: Eerdmans, 1996.

Eadie, John. *A Commentary on the Greek Text of The Epistle of Paul To The Ephesians.* 2nd ed. New York: Robert Carter and Brothers, 1861.

Fitzmyer, Joseph A. *The Letter to Philemon.* Anchor Bible. New York: Doubleday, 2000.

Fowl, Stephen E. *Ephesians: A Commentary.* New Testament Library; Louisville: Westminster John Knox, 2012.

Harris, Murray J. *Exegetical Guide to The Greek New Testament: Colossians and Philemon.* Nashville: B&H Academic, 2010.

Heil, John Paul. *Ephesians: Empowerment to Walk in Love for the Unity of All in Christ.* Atlanta: Society of Biblical Literature, 2007.

Hodge, Charles. *A Commentary on The Epistle To The Ephesians.* New York: Robert Corter & Brothers, 1878.

Hoehner, Harold W. *Ephesians: An Exegetical Commentary.* Grand Rapids: Baker Academic, 2002.

Larkin, William J. *Ephesians: A Handbook on The Greek Text.* Waco, TX: Baylor University Press, 2009.

Lincoln, Andrew T. *Ephesians.* Word Biblical Commentary 42. Dallas, TX: Word, 1990.

Lohse, Eduard. *Colossians and Philemon.* Philadelphia: Fortress, 1971.

Muddiman, John. *The Epistle to The Ephesians.* Peabody, MA: Hendrickson, 2004.

Schnackenburg, Rudolf. *The Epistle to The Ephesians.* Edinburgh: T&T Clark, 1991.

Talbert, Charles H. *Ephesians and Colossians.* Paideia. Grand Rapids: Baker Academic, 2007.

Turner, Samuel Hulbeart. *The Epistle to the Ephesians: In Greek and English, with an Analysis and Exegetical Commentary.* New York: Dean and Company, 1856.

Verhey, Allen and Joseph S. Harvard. *Ephesians.* Belief: A Theological Commentary on the Bible. Louisville: Westminster John Knox, 2011.

Wilberforce, A. Bertrand. *A Devout Commentary on The Epistle to the Ephesians.* Saint Louis, MO: B. Herder, 1902.

Williamson, Peter S. *Ephesians*. Catholic Commentary on Sacred Scripture. Grand Rapids: Baker Academic, 2009.

Witherington, Ben. *Letters And Homilies for Hellenized Christians. Volume 1. A Socio-Rhetorical Commentary on Titus, 1–2 Timothy and 1–3 John*. Downers Grove, IL: InterVarsity Press, 2006.

LEXICONS AND GRAMMARS

Baur, W., F. W. Danker, W. F. Arndt, and F. W. Gingrich. *Greek-English Lexicon of the New Testament and Other Early Christian Literature*. 3rd ed. Chicago: University of Chicago Press, 1999.

Blass, F., and A. Debrunner. *A Greek Grammar of the New Testament and Other Early Christian Literature*. Translated and revised by R. W. Funk. Chicago: University of Chicago Press, 1961.

Brooks, James A. and Carlton L. Winbery. *Syntax of New Testament Greek*. Lanham, MD: University Press of America, 1979.

Brown, Colin, ed. *New International Dictionary of New Testament Theology*. 4 vols. Grand Rapids: Zondervan, 1975–1985.

Campbell, Constantine R. *Basics of Verbal Aspect in Biblical Greek*. Grand Rapids: Zondervan, 2008.

Kittel, G. and G. Friedrich, eds. *Theological Dictionary of the New Testament*. Translated by G. W. Bromiley. 10 vols. Grand Rapids: Eerdmans, 1964–1976.

Machen, J. G. *New Testament Greek for Beginners*. Toronto, ON: Macmillan, 1923.

Moule, C. F. D. *An Idiom Book of New Testament Greek*. Cambridge: Cambridge University Press, 1953.

Porter, Stanley E. "A Functional Letter Perspective: Towards a Grammar of Epistolary Form." Pages 9–32 in *Paul and the Ancient Letter Form*. Edited by Stanley E. Porter and Sean A. Adams. Leiden: Brill, 2010.

Wallace, Daniel B. *Greek Grammar Beyond The Basics: An Exegetical Syntax of the New Testament*. Grand Rapids: Zondervan, 1996.

STUDIES

Arnold, Clinton. "Sceva, Solomon, and Shamanism: The Jewish Roots of the Problem at Colossae." *Journal of the Evangelical Theological Society* 55 (2012): 7–26.

Ameringer, Thomas Edward. *A Study in Greek Rhetoric*. Washington, DC: Catholic University of America, 1921.

Baugh, S. M. "A Foreign World: Ephesus in the First Century." Pages 13–52 in *Women in the Church: A Fresh Analysis of 1 Timothy 2:9–15*. Edited by Andreas J. Köstenberger and others. Grand Rapids: Baker Academic, 1995.

Berding, Kenneth. *What Are Spiritual Gifts? Rethinking the Conventional View.* Grand Rapids: Kregel, 2007.

Black, Stephanie L. *Sentence Conjunctions in the Gospel of Matthew: καί, δέ, τότε, γάρ, οὖν and Asyndeton in Narrative Discourse.* Journal for the Study of the New Testament Supplement Series 216. Studies in New Testament Greek 9. Sheffield: Sheffield Academic Press, 2002.

Bonard, Jody A. *The Mysticism of Hebrews: Exploring the Role of Jewish Apocalyptic Mysticism in the Epistle to the Hebrews.* Wissenshaftliche Untersuchungen zum Neuen Testament 2/331. Tübingen: Mohr Siebeck, 2012.

Bratcher, R. G. and E. A. Nida. *A handbook on Paul's letter to the Ephesians.* NY: United Bible Societies, 1993.

Brown, Raymond E. *An Introduction to The New Testament.* NY: Doubleday, 1997.

Bruce, F. F. "St. Paul in Rome: 4. The Epistle to the Ephesians." *Bulletin of the John Rylands Library Manchester* 49 (1967): 303–322.

Comfort, Philip Wesley. *A Commentary on the Manuscripts and Text of the New Testament.* Grand Rapids: Kregel Academic, 2015.

Comfort, Philip W. and David P. Barrett, eds. *The Text of The Earliest New Testament Greek Manuscripts: New and Complete Transcriptions with Photographs.* Wheaton, IL: Tyndale House, 2001.

Cozart, Richard M. *This Present Triumph: An Investigation into the Significance of the Promise of a New Exodus of Israel in the Letter to the Ephesians.* Eugene, OR: Wipf & Stock, 2013.

Culy, Martin M. "Double Case Constructions in Koine Greek." *Journal of Greco-Roman Christianity and Judaism* 6 (2009), 82–106.

Culy, Martin M., Mikeal C. Parsons, and Joshua J. Stigall. *Luke: A Handbook on the Greek Text.* Waco, TX: Baylor University Press, 2010.

de Hoop, Raymond, Marjo C. A. Korpel, and Stanley E. Porter, eds. *The Impact of Unit Delimitation on Exegesis.* Leiden: Brill, 2008.

DelHousaye, John. Review of Mikeal C. Parsons, Martin M. Culy, and Joshua J. Stigall, *Luke: A Handbook on the Greek Text, Review of Biblical Literature* [http://www.bookreviews.org] (2012).

Dupriez, Bernard. *A Dictionary of Literary Devices.* Translated by Albert W. Halsall. Toronto, ON: University of Toronto Press, 1991.

Epstein, Perle. *Kabbalah: The Way of the Jewish Mystic.* New York: Barnes and Noble, 1978.

Fitzmyer, Joseph A. and Daniel J. Harrington, eds. *A Manual of Palestinian Aramaic Texts.* Rome: Editrice Pontifices Istituto Biblico, 1994.

Fowl, Stephen E. *Ephesians: Being a Christian at Home and in the Cosmos.* Phoenix Guides to the New Testament 10. Sheffield: Sheffield Phoenix, 2014.

Grenfell, Bernard and Arthur S. Hunt, eds. *The Oxyrhunchus Papyri, Part 3.* London: Oxford University Press, 1903.

Goodrich, John K. *Paul as an Administrator of God in 1 Corinthians.* New York: Cambridge University Press, 2012.

Gorman, Michael J. *Elements of Biblical Exegesis: A Basic Guide for Students and Ministers.* Grand Rapids: Baker Academic, 2009.

Gosnell, Peter W. "Honor and Shame Rhetoric as a Unifying Motif in Ephesians." *Bulletin for Biblical Research* 16 (2006): 105–28.

Harril, Albert, J. *Slaves in the New Testament: Literary, Social, and Moral Dimensions.* Minneapolis: Fortress, 2006.

Hatch, Edwin and Henry A. Redpath. *A Concordance to The Septuagint and the other Greek versions of The Old Testament (Including the Apocryphal Books).* 3 vols. Grand Rapids: Baker Academic, 1991.

Heil, John Paul. Ephesians 5:18b: 'But Be Filled in the Spirit." *Catholic Biblical Quarterly* 69 (2007): 506–16.

Hobson, G. Thomas. "ἀσελγεία in Mark 7:22." *Filologia Neotestamentaria* 21 (2008): 65–74.

Jong, Leo. "Kavanah." Pages 123–30 in *Jewish Tradition in The Diaspora: Studies in Memory of Professor Walter J. Fischel.* Edited by Michael Maswari Caspi. Berkley, CA: Judah L. Magness Memorial Museum, 1981.

Kadushin, Max. *Worship and Ethics: A Study in Rabbinic Judaism.* Binghampton, NY: Global Publications, 2001.

Longman, Tremper. "Merism." Pages 464–66 in *Dictionary of The Old Testament: Wisdom, Poetry & Writings.* Ed. by Tremper Longman and Peter Enns. Downers Grove, IL: InterVarsity Press, 2008.

Murphy-O'Connor, Jerome. *St. Paul's Ephesus: Texts and Archaeology.* Collegeville, MN: Liturgical Press, 2008.

Noll, Mark A. *The Rise of Evangelicalism: The Age of Edwards, Whitefield and the Wesleys.* Downers Grove, IL: InterVarsity Press, 2003.

Oropeza, B. J. *Jews, Gentiles, and the Opponents of Paul: The Pauline Letters.* Eugene, OR: Cascade, 2012.

Pasqueli, G. *Storia della tradizione e critica del testo.* 2nd ed. Florence: Olscchky, 1971.

Rodgers, Peter R. "The Allusion to Genesis 2:23 at Ephesians 5:30." *Journal of Theological Studies* 41 (1990): 92–94.

Ryken, Leland. *The Devotional Poetry of Donne, Herbert, and Milton.* Wheaton, IL: Crossway, 2014.

Stowers, Stanley K. *Letter Writing in Greco-Roman Antiquity.* Louisville: Westminster John Knox Press, 1986.

Wenkel, David H. "The 'Breastplate of Righteousness' in Ephesians 6:14." *Tyndale Bulletin* 58 (2007): 275–87.

Wesley, Timothy L. *The Politics of Faith During The Civil War*. Baton Rouge, LA: Louisiana State University Press, 2013.

White, L. M. "Urban Development and Social Change in Imperial Ephesos." Pages 27–79 in *Ephesos: Metropolis of Asia*. Edited by H. Köster. Harvard Theological Studies 41. Valley Forge, PA: Trinity International, 1995.

Whitters, Mark F. "'The Eye Is the Lamp of the Body': Its Meaning in the Sermon on the Mount." *Irish Theological Quarterly* 71 (2006): 77–88.

Wink, Walter. *Naming The Powers: The Language of Power in the New Testament*. Philadelphia: Fortress, 1984.

Yee, T. –L. N. *Jews, Gentiles and Ethnic Reconciliation: Paul's Jewish Identity and Ephesians*. Society for New Testament Studies Monograph Series 130. Cambridge: Cambridge University Press, 2005.

Yeo, Khiok-khng. *Rhetorical Interaction in 1 Corinthians 8 & 10: A Formal Analysis with Preliminary Suggestions for a Chinese, Cross-Cultural Hermeneutic*. Leiden: Brill, 1995.

Zerbe, G. "Paul on the Human Being as a 'Psychic Body': Neither Dualist nor Monist." *Direction* 37 (2008): 168–84.

Scripture Index

AUTHOR INDEX

GRAMMAR INDEX

LITERARY / RHETORICAL INDEX

NOTES

NOTES

<u>NOTES</u>

NOTES

Made in the USA
Middletown, DE
18 October 2022